FLY FISHING THE INSHORE WATERS

LEFTY KREH

THE LYONS PRESS
Guilford, Connecticut
An imprint of The Globe Pequot Press

The Lyons Press is an imprint of The Globe Pequot Press.

10 9 8 7 6 5 4 3 2 1

Manufactured in the United States of America
ISBN: 1-58574-605-3

The Library of Congress Cataloguing-in-Publication Data is available on file.

CONTENTS

INTRODUCTION

Because of their long and well-deserved popularity among fly fishermen, earlier in the Library I devoted an entire volume to fly fishing for only three saltwater fish, the three great warm-water trophy species: bonefish, permit, and tarpon.*

But as saltwater fly fishing continues its dramatic growth in the United States, more and more anglers are now focusing their attention on many other saltwater species, and I want to explore this type of fishing with you.

Of course, the giant billfish — primarily the sailfish and marlin that inhabit the deep offshore waters around the world — have also become popular with a very small number of fly fishermen who have the interest (and, more important, the money) to pursue these giant gamefish.

But at the risk of offending my friends who enjoy fly rodding for billfish, I have to say that while it is an exciting sport with its own particular thrills, from a technique standpoint, as far as I am concerned, it's really not such a big deal. Frankly, anyone can do it, provided he or she can find a captain and mate who have mastered the art of teasing billfish up close to the stern of the boat; has enough arm and wrist strength to handle a 11 to 13-weight rod; and can deliver a saltwater streamer in a wide-looping, 25-foot lob cast (really a lazy and very poor cast) in the vicinity of the billfish's mouth.

Heck, when you really think about it, the most skilled performers in this type of fishing are not the anglers but the

---

Fly Fishing for Bonefish, Permit & Tarpon.

captain of the boat and his mate. The captain has to locate the billfish and place the boat on a proper course and speed to attract the fish. Then the mate, following directions from the captain, has to make the critical presentation and retrieve of the teaser rig that will bring the billfish up to the surface behind the boat in a frenzy to eat almost anything in sight. I've even seen such teased billfish attack the stern of the boat! And it's the mate who has to make the critical decision about when to remove the teaser from the water and when to tell the angler to lob cast the streamer that is going to become a substitute for the teaser in the billfish's frenzied mind.

Plus, in a typical day of fly fishing for billfish, you'll find that a lot of your time will be spent simply sitting on your butt watching the teaser being trolled behind the boat. Speaking for myself, I decided a long time ago that trolling for fish like this was just not how I wanted to spend my fishing days.

But there's no question that the hook-up and initial run of a giant billfish on a fly rod is a great adventure, and if it sounds like something you might want to try, then shoot, go for it! But I don't believe there's much more I can tell you about the techniques of fly fishing for billfish that you won't pick up from the captain and mate of a good billfishing boat in your first hour with them. However, I have provided a few tips on billfishing tackle and fly patterns in a short Appendix to this book. Otherwise, that's all you'll find about billfishing here.

I believe what's far more important, for most of our Library members, is whatever help I can give you in developing the knowledge and skills to fly fish for the numerous and very sporty saltwater species that inhabit the inshore waters close to the shorelines of our tropical and temperate saltwater seas.

Fly fishing for saltwater inshore fish may possibly be the fastest growing segment of our sport today. I think a princi-

Rob Fordyce and Lefty enjoy a day of snook fishing. ➤

pal reason for the growing popularity of fly fishing to these species is that, unlike the hatchery fish that are the only sport fish now readily available in many of our freshwater streams, inshore saltwater fish are *wild*, possessing the great stealth and strength that wildness provides. And they are readily accessible at modest cost to all fly fishermen throughout a huge range of our coastal waters.

Such growth and popularity require more attention among fly fishermen today. So that's what this book is designed to do. In the following pages, I will concentrate on developing your techniques and tactics for fly fishing to the principal inshore saltwater species — striped bass, albacore, redfish, bluefish, snook, barracuda, and sharks.

* * * * *

Inshore saltwaters offer a host of environments. Seatrout, redfish, and drum, for example, often inhabit grass-covered basins or flats where the water can average from a few inches to 20 feet in depth.

Snook (and its first cousin, the Australian barramundi) cruise shallow flats and hang around structure, from which they can dart out and ambush their prey. Favorite hiding places are around drowned trees and roots and near boat docks, old pilings, and shoreline banks that have been undercut by eroding tidal flows.

Striped bass can be found in many habitats, virtually any clean saltwater holding their food sources. Stripers spend time in the swirling water and foam among the rocks of a rugged shoreline, the waves pounding and crashing against these stone barriers. They will also cruise a calm, shallow flat. And they can often be found in waters as deep as 100 feet.

One of the most exciting fish you'll ever catch on a flat is a big shark. Since sharks can't tolerate cold water, flats warmed by the tropical sun are the places to seek them.

Redfish can be as frustrating as striped bass as far as locating them and then getting them to take your fly are concerned. I have seen reds cruising in waters so shallow that their backs stick up into the air. But they will seek a deep channel during a cold spell. And like striped bass, there are times when they seem totally uninterested in taking anything you offer them. While redfish don't normally hang around structure, if you can locate their food in water at the right temperature, you'll improve your chances of finding them.

There are a number of ways that you can fish the inshore waters. None is more interesting and exciting than sight fishing. This is done by either wading the shallow flats; anchoring and waiting for fish to come to you; drifting slowly in a boat over areas that hold fish; or having someone pole you in a boat designed for flats fishing.

In sight fishing, you search for fish, make an approach once you've seen them, and then cast. This sounds simple, but there are a lot of variables involved. Why God seems so often to place fish upwind of fly fishermen is something we will never understand. And when making presentations from a boat, you must always be aware that both the boat and the fish are *moving.* Casting and properly presenting a fly in these conditions are a timed art: not only do you have to cast into the breeze, you have to make the cast soon enough and long enough, and you also have to plan for the movement of the boat and fish so that your fly falls to the water exactly where you intended to place it.

So just as our other major fly-fishing trophy fish — trout, steelhead, salmon, bonefish, permit, and tarpon — require the development of special skills, techniques, and tactics, so too do the inshore saltwater species.

Overleaf: *Phil Lofgren releasing a freshly caught albacore.*

CHAPTER ONE

FINDING FISH INSHORE

Inshore fishing can mean fishing beaches and in bays, grass-covered basins, or backcountry, such as Melville and Bathurst islands in the Pacific or the area that stretches along the west coast of Florida from Naples to the Keys. This type of fishing includes the channels and bays that harbor bluefish, mackerel, jack crevalle, trevally, and seatrout, to name a few of the numerous species that inhabit these waters. Then there are the tropical flats of Florida and the Carribean that are the favored waters of permit, tarpon, bonefish, and redfish, and the cool-water flats of the Atlantic and Pacific coasts where striped bass roam in search of food. Inshore saltwaters offer a great variety of habitat types.

In such habitats, there are many times in saltwater fly fishing when it is absolutely vital to see the fish before you cast to it. In fact, what makes saltwater fly fishing so exciting is that much of it is visual — you see the fish before you make the cast, and then you watch it take your fly. And in many saltwater fishing circumstances, the sooner the fish can be located the better, as this gives the fly fisherman the decided sporting advantage of having ample time to determine where to throw his fly. To see fish quickly is therefore a skill the inshore fly fisherman must develop for success. Fortunately, there are tricks and techniques to help the angler.

Seeing a fish before you make a cast is either a great advantage or essential to success, both inshore and offshore. Two natural conditions help defeat anglers from seeing the quarry. One is wind. But other than trying to find a lee shore, there is little you can do about water that has been roiled with sediment stirred by the wind, or a surface that is so distorted you can't see beneath it.

The other condition that reduces your chances of seeing fish is surface glare. This you can do something about, if you have the proper tools. Fortunately, these are few in number.

First, if you fish and don't wear a hat, you are at a distinct disadvantage. Try this simple experiment. Wearing no hat, stand in an elevated position above the water on a bright sunny day and look down at the bottom. You will see some detail on

Hat with Underbrim Darkened with Shoe Polish

the bottom. Now put on a hat with a brightly colored underbrim. You will see more bottom detail. Finally, put on a hat that shades the eyes and has a dark underbrim. You will find that you are able to see much more bottom detail.

I recommend wearing this last type of hat. The color of the underside of the brim is very important; it should be black in color, or very dark. A hat with a light underbrim reflects the light bouncing off the water and directs it into the eyes, reducing your chances of seeing well.

I do not like the very long-brimmed hats, however, for I believe accurate casting requires being able to see the line as it unrolls in the air toward the fish, and an elongated hat brim hides much of this important motion from your vision.

SUNGLASSES

Polaroids or polarized sunglasses are essential for seeing fish in saltwater because they reduce glare and increase contrast. There are two basic types of polarized glasses. One is simply a polarizing screen sandwiched between two pieces of soft clear plastic. This is the least expensive type, and as long as these sunglasses remain in good condition they work well. However, they scratch easily, and most fishermen go through many pairs before they elect to buy the second, and better, type of polarized sunglasses. These consist of a polarizing screen between two clear pieces of hardened plastic.

If you wear prescription glasses, you also have two choices for sunglasses. You can purchase clip-ons, which are frameless polarized lenses that you attach to the frames holding your prescription lenses. I've never found any clip-ons that were totally satisfactory, however. All I've tried are of the soft plastic type that scratch easily. And when I'm traveling in a fast-running boat, the wind can blow them off.

Most fly fishermen who need glasses and who are serious about their sport eventually elect the second option and purchase a pair of the much more expensive prescription-ground polarized glasses. Once they try these, they don't want to go back to clip-ons.

If you see poorly up close but your distance vision is pretty good, you may want to buy a pair of glasses that feature a tiny magnifier in the bottom of each lens. The rest of the lens on this type of glasses is a polarized sheet protected on each side by optical glass.

There are three standard tints of polarized sunglasses: brown/amber, blue/gray, and yellow. *For most fishing, I believe the brown/amber color is best.* This most common tint for glasses is sometimes referred to as "Cosmotan." On the flats and in the shallows, the brown/amber color seems to be the most effective. If you have only one pair of polarized glasses, this is perhaps the best color to buy.

But if you fish offshore, blue/gray seems to penetrate the surface better and is preferred by many experienced offshore skippers. Sunglasses in this tint certainly perform better for me. The same blue/gray glasses are also excellent for fishing vast, snow-white flats such as those encountered at Christmas Island. Almost all of the bottom at that island is brilliant white, and it is viewed under an equatorial sun. In such conditions, I find that my eyes tire more quickly unless I use these darker blue/gray polarized glasses.

There is a third tint for glasses that I find extremely helpful when light conditions are poor. On dark, overcast days when rain is threatening, yellow-tinted glasses (similar to those worn by skeet and trap shooters) are superb. Not all optical outlets sell these, but I suspect many more will in the future. The yellow builds contrast and helps separate objects when they are seen, much as shooting glasses do under poor light conditions. However, on sunlit days the bright yellow glasses create a considerable amount of eyestrain for me, so I avoid using them under such bright light conditions.

I understand one optical manufacturer is presently experimenting with clear polarized glasses, and these will likely offer real promise for special fishing situations.

Sideshields on the frames of your sunglasses are almost a necessity for fishing inshore waters and flats. They prevent the glare that bounces off the water at your side or behind you from striking the inside of your glasses and affecting your ability to see well. You can make your own sideshields from a variety of products, but several companies now sell super-tough sideshields. Other companies have built sideshields into the frame — a commendable idea.

Also, since polarized glasses are manufactured to eliminate glare under what are considered general light conditions, you can sometimes remove additional glare if you tilt your head left or right. Try this from time to time as you search for fish.

Keeping glasses clean is essential, and there are some tricks for doing this. Obviously, with soft-plastic polarized glasses, you want to store them in a soft protective case and take care when you put them down to avoid scratching. And if you let salt spray collect on the surface of the lenses and then use a napkin or cloth to remove the encrusted salt, the hardened salt crystals will often scratch the lenses. In such a situation, a little freshwater is needed to soften the crystals. Dip the glasses in the melted ice from the onboard cooler on your boat and then clean them. Or pick up a small bottle of lens cleaner at almost any drugstore or optical store. These bottles are easy to carry and contain the very best liquid for the purpose.

I have a fetish about keeping my glasses clean when fishing. If a drop of salt spray gets on them, I want to wipe it off immediately. This means carrying something to clean the glasses with, and the best thing I know of is a good, dry napkin. Trouble is, if you carry napkins in your pocket and it rains or salt spray gets to you or you start sweating, the napkins become useless. For that reason, I carry several napkins in a Ziploc bag in my shirt pocket.

Another vision problem frequently presents itself, especially when you're landing a fish. The fish is finally brought to the boat, you bend over, and just before you pick it up, the fish beats the surface wildly with its tail, splashing water all over your glasses. The water never seems to drain off quickly enough, and you can't see.

But I have a solution for this, too. There is a product on the market that is applied to a car windshield to cause water to bead up and run off the glass. In all but the heaviest rains, this material will flush water so quickly from the windshield that you really don't need your wipers. The brand I prefer for my glasses is called Rain-X, which is obtainable from many auto parts stores.

To use Rain-X, clean your polarized glasses, then put a little of the Rain-X liquid on a piece of napkin or cloth and apply it to the surface of the glasses. It disappears from sight within seconds. One manufacturer, Specialized Eyewear, that applies Teflon coating to its lenses to deter dirt from accumulating reports that Rain-X will eventually remove the Teflon coating on glasses. But on all other eyeglasses I have worn, Rain-X works wonders for me.

Finally, almost any fly fisherman who fishes in warmer climates and wears glasses or sunglasses finds them constantly slipping down his nose. There are devices you can attach to the rear of the frames that will hold the glasses tightly against your head, but I find these uncomfortable. So I have come up with a simple system that keeps my glasses sitting on my nose exactly where I want them. They can also be readjusted quickly and easily to another position.

Flats fishing off the coast of Key West. ➤

Attach a short length of string (I use old fly line) to each frame. Then sew one side of a strip of Velcro to one string and the other side to the other string. Position the glasses where you want them, then simply put the Velcro sections together to hold the glasses firmly where you placed them.

THE APPEARANCE OF FISH IN SALTWATER

Perhaps the first thing to realize when you're sight fishing inshore is that in saltwater you should really not be looking for something that looks like a fish at all. To give you an example, some typical flats' species, such as trevally, permit, tarpon, and bonefish, have silver sides that act just like a mirror, reflecting the environment or bottom the fish are swimming over. It is hard to believe that very large permit, bonefish, or trevally swimming in three feet of water can be nearly invisible. But along the top of the back and the edge of the forked tail on a trevally or permit there is a thin, dark line that looks like a dark, horizontal "Y." This is what the fisherman should watch for. The size of a 30-pound trevally or permit almost always astonishes the angler who catches it and lifts it from the water, when he remembers that all he saw at first was a thin black line knifing through the water.

As another example, we all know that a bonefish is a very difficult fish to see. Often it is the large eye, the slightly pale green or blue tail, a shadow beneath the fish, or the slightly darker shading of its back that is visible. And a bonefish is almost always easier to locate if it is swimming toward you rather than at a right angle to you. When a bonefish is swimming toward you, you are looking at the back of the fish, which is usually somewhat darker than the side. When a bonefish swims at a right angle to you, you are looking at the mirror-like side, which reflects the bottom.

So while it can sometimes also be the case in freshwater streams, in saltwater particularly you should not expect to see an entire fish.

When you're seeking silvery-sided fish that frequent the inshore shallows, it is often best to search on bright days for the shadow the fish casts on the bottom. And the higher the fish are above the bottom, the larger the shadow.

LOCATING FISH IN SHALLOW SALTWATER

Searching for the inshore species in shallow water is some-what different from searching for fish in deep water. *When fish are in water less than a foot deep, you should look at the surface.* A fish of catchable size will produce a wake, usually in the form of one or more "V"s, when it swims in less than a foot of water. Remember that this wake will usually be two or three feet *behind* the fish. This means that on your presentation you should throw the fly farther ahead of the wake than you might normally think you should.

When fish swim in water more than a foot deep, you should look at the bottom. This is because no wake is produced by fish swimming close to the bottom, unless the fish are very large. This sounds reasonable, but many fishermen simply don't follow this advice.

Let me give you an analogy. If you look in a store window at items just inside the window, you see nothing farther back inside the store. But if you look through the window at the back of the store, anyone moving between you and the back would interrupt your vision and be noticed.

So in inshore fishing, when you concentrate upon look-ing at the bottom, you will see any fish that moves between you and the bottom. It's a hard trick to master but essential for becoming a good fly fisherman in shallow saltwater.

The angle of the sun can have a decided effect on the glare on the surface of the water. And in turn, this will have an important effect upon how well you will be able to see fish. So as you move along, try to keep the sun behind you (or at least to the side and slightly behind you) when you are searching for fish in the shallows. If the sun is in front of you, there will be so much glare that you may find yourself fishing blind.

Try to avoid moving across the water toward a bright cloud on the horizon. The cloud will reflect off the surface as white glare and prevent you from seeing anything at all. Conversely, if the light is poor, approaching fish along a shoreline with dark green foliage in the background will often allow you to see better below the surface of the water.

The time of year may also influence how well you see fish in the inshore shallows. The best viewing light is available under a cloud-free sky when the sun is *high overhead*. The lower the angle of the sun, the more difficult it is to see into the water. One reason Christmas Island is so ideal for bone-fishing is because it is located on the equator; the sun is high above the horizon for most of the day.

And fly fishermen who travel during the winter months to tropical locales such as Florida, the Bahamas, or other points far from the equator may be disappointed with the light conditions and how they affect their fishing. In the winter months the sun simply doesn't get high enough for good viewing until about 9:00 in the morning; and by 4:00 in the afternoon the lower sun angle makes seeing difficult again. But in these same areas in the summer months, you can fish two or three hours earlier and later because of the higher sun angles the summer season provides.

If you are fishing from a boat, try not to stare at the water. You'll see little. And constantly scan the area; don't just concentrate on the waters in front of you! Frequently examine the water as far away as you feel you can locate fish. Look for redfish, for example, at a distance of at least 50 yards around the boat. With sharks, which often break the water's surface with their dorsal fin and tail as they swim along, you can look as far as 200 yards from the boat. When wading the shallows, try to look as far ahead as it is possible to see fish.

Swimming fish often cause a disturbance on the surface. Tiny ripples in a calm area ("nervous water") mean fish are swimming underneath. Or if the waves in the water are mostly coming from one direction and you perceive one wave coming from an entirely different direction, a swimming fish may be the cause.

On a shallow flat, a difference in bottom coloration can indicate a good area to look for fish. Snook, barramundi, barracuda, and other inshore species enjoy lying in white sand holes on a flat, so check these out carefully. Also check dark spots. Logs, coral heads, and debris on a flat are often ambush spots or hideouts for many species.

Look for muddy places, too. Redfish, seatrout, snapper, ladyfish, jack crevalle, mullet, and other species of fish will often try to root out crabs or shrimp from the bottom, creating small puffs of mud that are frequently visible as they rise to the surface of the water. When you observe these puffs, attempt to present and retrieve your fly around the edges of the freshest of them, those that appear to have been the most recently made.

Various types of rays can also be helpful for locating gamefish. Typically, a ray will cruise along and then drop to the bottom and pound its wings against the bottom to flush out the tiny food creatures hiding there. Because rays are relatively slow swimmers, many faster-swimming fish hover nearby and rush in and grab the fleeing shrimp, crabs, and other morsels before the ray can reach them. And even when rays are not pounding the bottom in this manner, many predatory fish will continue to swim alongside them. I once saw a manta ray in northern Australia accompanied by a cobia that had to weigh nearly 100 pounds! So anytime you see a ray pounding the bottom or swimming, be sure to check it out. The fish attending the ray will be in a feeding mood and will be well placed for your cast.

At night, lighted docks, bridges, and channel markers attract small bait and shrimp, which in turn draw predatory fish, especially snook. Learning to see these fish is easy and can produce some excellent fishing. Keep in mind that in these conditions *predatory fish will always hold on the uptide side of the lighted area.* For example, if the tide is flowing from north to south, the predators will be on the north side. To locate the fish, study the spot where the shadow line produced by the lights falls on the water. The fish will be just inside that line, facing into the current so that they can grab any drifting bait, shrimp, or crabs before they reach the structure. By standing on the bridge or climbing up on the structure in the water, you can often see these fish, which will resemble a dark shadow within the shadows. Once you know what you are looking for, they are really quite easy to see.

In deeper inshore waters, birds are frequently a terrific aid to finding fish. Gulls, terns, and flocks of other water birds will often pluck shrimp and baitfish pushed to the surface by predators below. When you spot water birds exhibiting that behavior, it's almost always a sure sign that inshore sportfish are under the baitfish, feeding.

Also, many fish are frequently spooked by a bird passing overhead and will make an abrupt underwater movement that will disturb the surface of the water. When you spot such a movement, wait a bit, as the spooked fish will soon settle down. Then slowly and carefully approach the area where the water was formerly disturbed and make your presentation.

Even a flock of birds just resting on the surface can be a good indicator of predatory fish below. The birds may be aware of a large school of bait beneath them and therefore be waiting for predatory fish to come along and begin feeding and pushing the baitfish upward. If you have no place special to go, it may be worth your while to hang around. Birds are fine indicators of the presence of tuna, albacore, bluefish, and, often, striped bass.

Watch for small oil slicks as well. The bodies of many baitfish contain a great deal of oil. When predatory fish such as dogtooth tuna, mackerel, and bluefish cut and chop into the baitfish well below the surface, this oil is released and forms a slick on top of the water.

White splashes on the horizon generally indicate leaping fish. After all, something had to make that splash!

When you think about it, there are really only a few places in saltwater where small fish can hide from predators. Floating debris, such as trees, logs, boards, and old boxes, as well as large patches of grass, are many times the only hiding places available to small baitfish. So *always* check debris for fish. Inshore markers and buoys are other good locations to check. Tripletail love to hang around such structures, as do cobia and snook.

There are many tricks to locating fish. Fortunately, most of them are easy to learn. Learning to see fish is essential to becoming a good inshore fly fisherman.

OVERLEAF: *Low tide at Philbin Beach on Martha's Vineyard.*

CHAPTER TWO

UNDERSTANDING THE TIDES

One of the greatest differences between fresh and saltwater fishing is the effect that tides have on fishing success. If you want to be proficient in saltwater, you need to have at least a basic understanding of the tides and how they operate.

The tide is the rise and fall of water. In any location affected by tide, this rise and fall causes the height of the water to change and also produces a current flow. Both of these effects are very important to fish and fishermen.

TIDE CHANGES

While there are more than 50 reasons for the rise and fall of tide, the major cause is the gravitational pull of the moon and sun on the earth and its waters. A less important reason to consider, particularly where the water is shallow, is the presence of wind. I'll discuss the effects of wind on the tide a little later in the book.

Let's first look at tidal action as it occurs on a monthly basis. During each 28-day period throughout the year, there are four major tide changes in most locations around the world. For the first seven days of that period, there is little rise and fall in the water. Then come seven more days in which the tide rises

Tides and Phases of the Moon

much higher and falls much lower every day. Then there is another seven-day period when waters rise and fall only a little. In the last seven days, waters again have a large rise and fall. *The first and third seven-day periods when the tide rises and falls only a little are called "neap" (pronounced "nip") tides. The second and fourth seven-day periods when tides rise much higher and fall much lower are called "spring" tides.* Some people remember this by saying the tides "spring up and down."

Local newspapers in most coastal communities give a daily listing of the local tidal rise and fall and of the neap and spring tides occurring. Many fishing publications provide the same sort of information. But there is a simple way to tell whether a spring tide or neap tide is occurring no matter where you are fishing. Just look at the moon. If there is a full moon or no moon, then maximum gravitational pull is being placed on the earth and spring tides that rise and fall considerably are being created. If there is a quarter moon, gravitational pull is diminished and neap tides will be occurring.

How does this help you as a saltwater fly fisherman? First, understand that tides repeat themselves *every two weeks!* For example, let's assume that you were at Lucky Ledge Light on Sunday the 10th and fishing was terrific, especially at noon. If you came back the next Sunday at noon and tried fishing, you would find the tidal phase to be almost exactly the opposite and you would probably have poor success. But if you came back the Sunday after that, tidal conditions would be almost identical to those of your first trip, unless a major weather change had intervened and interfered with these normal tidal phases. Remember, *the tidal phase is generally repeated every two weeks.*

Looking at this tidal phenomenon on a daily basis, there are a few places in the world where only one low tide and one high tide occur per day. And in rare places such as Fiji there is no real tide at all. But in most places in the world, *saltwater fishermen can count on four tides during a 24-hour period — two highs and two lows.* Approximately every six hours you will see a change from either a falling or rising tide. For example, the tide will fall for about six hours. Then the tide will rise for about six hours, then fall again.

Next, it is important to recognize that *tides occur about one hour later each day.* Thus, if a high tide occurred at 10:00 a.m. today, tomorrow that high tide will be at 11:00 a.m.

All of the above explanations of monthly and daily actions depend upon the weather conditions staying approximately the same. Wind, for example, can have a major effect on the flow and height of water in an area, regardless of whether there is a neap or spring tidal phase.

In areas where there is a lot of shallow water, especially a large basin (Currituck Sound in North Carolina is a good example), wind blowing strongly from one direction can actually push or shove a lot of the water downwind. For instance, if a stiff wind is blowing from the west for a day or two, the water on the east side of a shallow bay may rise several feet higher than it would in calm conditions. Meantime, the west side of the basin may have little or no water. So while wind is usually not a major factor in tidal rise and fall, it can have an effect often enough that the fisherman should be aware of it.

Here are some important points to remember about tides:

1. The tide that rises and falls very little and lasts for seven days is called a neap tide. In the seven days following a neap tide, the water will rise much higher and fall much lower. This is a spring tide.

2. The moon can indicate whether a neap or spring tide is occurring. During quarter moon phases, neap tides occur. During the dark of the moon or when there is a full moon, spring tides occur.

3. Tide conditions usually repeat themselves every two weeks.

4. Tides occur roughly one hour later each day, so plan your fishing accordingly.

HOW TIDES AFFECT YOUR FISHING SUCCESS

One way the tide affects fishing is through flooding areas that fish normally can't get to. For example, shallow flats on a low tide either are dry or have so little water that fish can't get up on them. But during a high tide, fish are able to swim onto the flats. Meanwhile, that same tide is also transporting the prey on which fish feed onto the flat; and its current often concentrates these food sources in particular areas. It's obvious that recognizing where and when these concentrations of prey occur can make a big difference in your fishing success.

This almost sounds like the title of a song (or maybe a book I ought to write someday), but here's something worth remembering: *Baitfish ain't got no home!* It is critical to an understand-

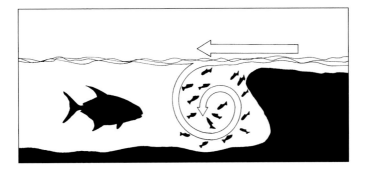

Vertical Eddy

ing of saltwater fly fishing to recognize that *many of the food sources saltwater species prey on do not live in specific locations but are instead carried by the tide.*

Compare this behavior to that of freshwater prey, which might be called "homebodies." In a freshwater stream, baitfish, worms, crayfish, sculpins, minnows, and other prey generally inhabit a particular pool. When rains swell the stream, these creatures seek shelter nearby to avoid being swept away from their home pool. In fact, most of them will live their entire lives and die in the same pool.

In saltwater, the very opposite is true. Most creatures preyed on by the predatory sportfish being sought by fly fishermen are nomads. Shrimp may be transported by the tide several miles in a given day. Mullet, menhaden, alewives, bay anchovies, and dozens of other saltwater baitfish are constantly changing their location. Crabs are forever being swept along with the current.

If the tide is flowing over a coral flat, oyster bar, or reef, there is likely a *vertical eddy* on the side of the reef that is downtide. The water on this side swirls somewhat like that of a water wheel in motion. Baitfish are momentarily trapped, and this in turn lures predatory fish.

Let me give you another example of how understanding the way tides function can mean more hook-ups. If the banks of a tidal creek or river are flooded at high tide, baitfish will seek shelter and food among the drowned trees. But when the tide begins to fall, the baitfish will eventually have to return to the river. Sensing that predators will be lurking close to shore waiting to eat them, the baitfish will not return until the last possible moment. The last water pouring off these drowned flats will run out through depressions, small creeks, and ditches, and these are the places the baitfish will choose to make their final exit and swim down into the river. So it's a good idea to fish on a falling tide at the mouth of any tidal creek or drainage ditch.

Many people think that an incoming tide is always the best for fishing. Of course, that's not always true. For example, suppose there is a flat rising from deep water to a ridge, and beyond the ridge is a large bay. Predatory fish will often feed up on this flat as the tide rises. And after the water is above the ridge, the predatory fish may well cross over the ridge and follow their prey, feeding all through the falling tide as it recedes into the bay beyond.

Feeding Spots at Mouth of Bay during Rising and Falling Tides

 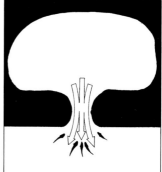

In a large basin or bay with a narrow neck connecting it to the main body of water, fishing may be excellent on both the incoming (rising) tide and the outgoing (falling) tide. On the incoming tide, the creatures that predators prey on will flow with the tidal current into the opening of the bay. The best feeding spot for predators will be on the *inside* of the mouth of the opening. Think of this as the opening of a funnel, through which the bait are carried from the larger body of water into the bay or basin. But as the tide falls, the predatory fish will move to the *outside* of the mouth of the opening and await the prey being swept out of the bay through the opening.

There are many situations where a *slack tide* (a tide with no current or rise and fall) can produce the best fishing conditions. This is particularly true when fishing for predatory species that prefer to hang around buoys, markers, and other such structures. When the tide is racing past a buoy, certain fish that live nearby, such as snook, tripletail, cobia, and jewfish, will simply hug the bottom and avoid fighting the tidal current. But when the tide goes slack, these fish will often rise and hold near the buoy. This is the time to fish for them.

Tides can also have a major impact on the *water temperature* in an area, and in turn, on the behavior and feeding habits of the predatory fish in the area. Here are a few examples of this phenomenon at work.

In many coastal locations, during the warmer months the sun will beat down on the standing water in a shallow bay. If the bay bottom is black or covered with dark turtle grass, this water will heat up rapidly, and to avoid discomfort, predatory fish may leave the area. But as a falling tide drains off this extra warm water from the bay and a rising tide brings in cooler water, the fish will often return to the cooler water to feed.

Conversely, in the Caribbean in the winter months, a cold front will often push very cold water onto the flats, causing the predatory fish to flee to deeper, warmer water.

Along the New England coast in early spring, one of the best places to fish for stripers is in bays where the bottom is very dark, creating rising water temperatures that attract the stripers from the cooler ocean water.

So as you plan your inshore fishing vacations, keep in mind such temperature variations and their effect upon the feeding habits of predatory fish. Where you can, it's preferable to travel to areas that contain shallow water closely abutting deep ocean water. Here's why. Suppose you are booked into a lodge that is located near large, shallow flats that predatory fish typically feed on but this lodge is well away from deep water. If a cold front arrives at the time you arrive, the water temperature on the flats is going to drop and the predatory fish are going to move a considerable distance away to seek deeper and warmer water. And they will likely stay down for several days. So much for your fishing!

But if you choose a lodge where the fishing flats are close to deep water, you need not worry so much about changes in water temperature during cold fronts. Since a cold front generally causes no dramatic changes in the temperature of deep ocean water, each incoming tide will bring in warmer water from that deep area, warming the water of the flats and maintaining an acceptable temperature for the predatory fish.

Tidal flow can have a major effect upon *water quality*, as well. If wind or other factors have dirtied the water so badly that fishing is well nigh impossible, you will not get much relief from the poor fishing conditions during neap tides. But during spring tides, so much water is sucked out of the area and is immediately replaced by clear water that fishing conditions will return to normal.

Along many shorelines and around mangroves and other trees that line the banks, all sorts of grass and floating debris will collect on a high tide. When the tide goes out, the grass and debris are left stranded on the banks. If another high tide rises high enough to refloat the grass and debris, fishing can get complicated. So much matter is floating on and in the water that it will spoil your retrieves. A fly fisherman who is aware of this problem can avoid areas in such conditions.

Where tidal currents flow rapidly through inlets and around projecting points of land, eddies are created, just as they are when a freshwater stream flows past a rock. Predatory fish will lie either in the eddy or along the edge of the quiet current, waiting for any prey species to be swept past them. Anglers will find it helpful to remember this.

Many people chum for a host of species in saltwater. Tidal phases can affect chumming success. Unless you are chumming fish up from considerable depths, a slack tide will usually produce poorly. This is because the chum that is placed overboard will fall almost vertically to the bottom — attracting few fish outside the immediate area. Or if the tide is running very slowly, the chum line will not spread out as far as you want and the number of fish alerted to your chum will be reduced. Or if the tide runs too rapidly, you'll need to use more chum to keep the chum slick from becoming too widespread or dissipated.

When fly fishing in a chum line, you need to use a sinking fly line. A sink-tip works well when the tide is running rather slowly, but you will need a faster-sinking line as the current speed increases.

The key to successful chumming is to keep your fly, lure, or bait drifting at the same depth and speed as the chum. This means constantly being aware of changes in tidal current and reacting appropriately to those changes.

To be a successful inshore fishermen, you must be aware of how tides affect the behavior of predatory fish.

OVERLEAF: *Pip Winslow casting to stripers off Martha's Vineyard.*

CHAPTER THREE

TACKLE FOR INSHORE FLY FISHING

The tackle needed for inshore fly fishing, of course, is determined to some degree by the species you seek. Obviously, you wouldn't use the same fly rod, line, and reel when fishing for small redfish that you would for big sharks. Fortunately, however, you don't need a large array of tackle.

RODS

The first requirement for selecting a rod is knowing which flies will be used. Most people first purchase a rod, then a line and reel, and finally some flies. That's the wrong way to go about it, because it is the selection of your flies and how they are cast that will largely determine what gear you need.

For most inshore fly-fishing situations, a rod that throws an 8 or a 9-weight line is the best all-around tool. A rod/line combination like this is perfect for snook, redfish, and striped bass, where large or heavy flies are not needed, and for perhaps 80 percent of all inshore fly fishing.

There are some inshore situations where a 10 or even 11-weight rod might be desirable. You would want a heavy stick like that if you were after cobia, which can be very strong. And when fishing inshore wrecks for amberjack, snapper, grouper, and other powerful fish, you need a heavy rod to help lift the fish away from the structure.

On the other hand, you might fish inshore for very small fish, such as white or yellow perch, mangrove snappers, smaller seatrout, or ladyfish, all species that do not demand heavy gear. A 5 or 6-weight rod is often the most pleasant choice, and some anglers opt for even lighter rods for these small species.

But in the main, an 8 or 9-weight rod will best serve the inshore saltwater fly fisherman.

One of the most important factors in rod selection is the size of the largest guide, which is called the butt or stripping guide. When the angler shoots fly line from the deck toward the target, the line reaches this butt guide in wavering coils and loops that have to be funneled through the guide. Once it passes through the butt guide, the line travels in a rather straight path. But the butt guide is the most important to line performance, as it is the conduit through which all the mess of line must first travel.

From years of experience I'm convinced that the *smallest-*size butt guide you should have on an inshore fly rod is a 20-mm. I much prefer larger than that. A 25-mm guide is better, and some experienced anglers even prefer one larger. Rod manufacturers are aware of the need for a large guide, but they must make rods that are esthetically pleasing and will be purchased by anglers. For that reason, few commercially manufactured rods come equipped with extra-large stripping guides. But any decent fly-rod shop has someone who can replace an existing smaller guide with a larger one for you.

One-foot ceramic guides are another issue in rod selection. After a lot of testing, I have concluded that a fly rod equipped with snake guides will perform better than one armed with all ceramic guides. My experience has shown that ceramic guides reduce the distance of a cast by about 10 percent. In fact, tournament casters, who actually measure their longer casts with a ruler, tried the ceramic guides when they first appeared but soon replaced them with the tried-and-true snake guides.

A few anglers have said that the new gel-spun backing lines, such as Spectra, Spiderwire, or Remington's Kevlar, wear guides badly. This is probably true. But considering the relatively few times that backing flows through the guides, I think most fishermen will agree that is not a critical point.

REELS

The selection of a saltwater fly reel is a much more important decision than the selection of a freshwater reel, since in many saltwater situations the larger size of these fish requires that the reel be more than a device for storing line; its storage capacity, its drag characteristics, the smoothness of its action are all critical performance aspects of a reel when you are fighting a large saltwater fish at great distances.

Of course, a saltwater reel must be able to resist the corrosive effects of salt. But many freshwater reels being manufactured today for steelhead, bass, or salmon fishing will do well for inshore fly fishing — providing you take reasonable care of them. I have used some freshwater Hardy reels, for example, in saltwater for more than 20 years. Admittedly, they're chipped and slightly eroded on the outside, but the innards are clean and work well. With reels that are not specifically made for saltwater fishing, a minimal amount of care will usually suffice.

Try to protect the reels from salt spray or immersion while fishing. When you return home, wash the outer surfaces with *warm* soapy water. Use an an old toothbrush to scour around the foot of the reel, where corrosion is more often visible.

Of course, if you can afford it, a reel with an adjustable drag is better than a reel that doesn't have this option.

To summarize, there is no question that a large-capacity reel with adjustable drag manufactured of materials that resist corrosion are preferable. But you really don't need those $400+ reels so many people feel are essential. Any reel that holds 150 yards of backing will handle almost any inshore fly fishing situation you will encounter, except angling for large tarpon and perhaps albacore.

LINES

I frequently hear, "I'm going to start fly fishing in saltwater. I guess I need a saltwater-taper line." And often people who fish for bonefish feel they should use a bonefish-taper. Others seeking tarpon may assume the correct fly line is a tarpon-taper. These choices of lines may be best for them. But there are several reasons why they may *not* want to select any one of these three specially tapered lines, and I will deal with these reasons in the section that follows.

The novice saltwater angler is confronted with such an array of fly lines that it's difficult to make a purchase. Even many experienced fly fishermen do not use the best lines for their particular fishing — or worse, use lines that actually restrict them from taking advantage of the full potential of their tackle. Maybe this would be a good place for me to try to clear up some of this confusion.

Fly lines are constructed in different tapers: level, double-taper, weight-forward, and shooting taper (more frequently called "shooting head"). For 99 percent of all saltwater fly fishing, the weight-forward and the shooting head are the only two tapers you will ever really need. In only rare situations is a double-taper or level line better than these two designs. So you can narrow your line choice down to these two tapers: weight-forward and shooting head.

Weight-Forward Lines

Weight-forward lines have a heavy belly section (the middle part of the taper), but the belly section is not a level line. The forward part of the belly tapers to a thinner diameter toward the front of the line. This front taper allows the fly to be placed more quietly on the water. Toward the rear of the thick belly section is a back taper, which makes a smooth transition from the heavy belly to the thinner shooting line.

The first 30 feet of any weight-forward fly line (minus a very short level section at the very front end of the line) is weighted, and the line is given a number which corresponds to that weight. Thus, the first 30 feet of a number 8 weight-forward line is 210 grains. Manufacturers are allowed a few grains' leeway either side of the specified weight. And they have the option to concentrate the weight toward the front end, the back end, or the middle of that 30 feet.

To make things even more confusing, a weight-forward line for short-range casting, for example, may be designed with a very thin belly section. However, a long-belly line to be used for distance casting, and bearing the same line number as the short-range line just mentioned, will have an extended heavy section to the rear of the first 30 feet. In other words, any properly manufactured number 8 weight-forward line must weigh about 210 grains for the first 30 feet, but the balance of the line may have a variety of diameters or configurations. Obviously, this means that a given selection of lines designated as number 8 weight-forward may cast very differently.

By now it should be very apparent that manufacturers need to come up with a better system of rating lines. If they did, they would probably sell more fly lines, and they would certainly better serve their customers.

The length of the front taper, the belly section, and the back taper determines what type of fishing the line is best suited for. The design of a weight-forward line will drastically influence the speed with which the cast can be made, how the line and leader perform during the casting motion, and how the fly lands on the water. The taper design also affects how well you can cast at short or long distances. You need to select a weight-forward line that suits your casting skills and the specific needs of your fishing situations.

For example, tarpon and bonefish-taper lines (as well as the saltwater-taper lines designed very much like them that you may want to consider for your inshore fly fishing) have a very short front taper, a heavy short belly, and a short back taper. All three of these lines should really be called short-range, speed-casting tapers. They are designed for short-range work, with the angler holding the fly and some of the line outside the rod to make a quick cast. But the heavy belly and short taper concentrate the weight near the front of the line, making the line and fly splash down rather heavily, often alerting the fish.

If your casting ability requires you to confine your inshore fishing to distances of no more than 50 feet, then these lines are fine. But when you locate fish at distances greater than 50 feet and are capable of casting well in, say, the 50 to 70-foot range or even farther, then you will do better with a conventional (or standard) weight-forward line. Such a conventional weight-forward design has a front and back taper and a thinner, longer belly section. With your advanced casting skills, you can still cast to the fish quickly, and the line will hit the water more quietly and present the fly more gently.

The saltwater, tarpon, and bonefish-taper lines have another disadvantage that often creates problems for fly fishermen. During the forward cast, the line is relatively straight behind the angler until the rod stops its forward motion. At that point, the line begins to unroll, starting at the rod tip. Meanwhile, *the line immediately outside the rod tip has to support the loop as the line unrolls toward the target.* The running line to the rear of the 30 feet of line of a saltwater, tarpon, or bonefish-taper is very thin. If a long cast is to be made, then a considerable length of this running line remains outside the rod tip during casting. This thin line is not stiff enough to unroll smoothly at the end of the forward cast when the stop is made, so it tends to collapse, causing shock waves and imperfections in the forward cast. This again is another reason why *saltwater, tarpon, and bonefish-taper lines are not the best choice for casting longer distances.*

In addition, the belly section of these three lines is quite large in diameter compared to that of other weight-forward lines. This means they will have greater air resistance, making a longer cast into a breeze more difficult.

If you cannot cast easily beyond 50 feet, you may want to use a saltwater, tarpon, or bonefish-taper. But realize that you are going to make sacrifices in presentation and distance. If you can cast beyond 50 feet, however, and you want to make a quieter presentation, or if you need to cast longer distances, then a conventional weight-forward line, or perhaps even a weight-forward line to which an extra long belly has been added, will perform better for you.

Shooting Heads

One of the difficulties in saltwater fly fishing is getting the fly to swim through a considerable amount of water. The sea is such a big place, and many species we fish for are constantly on the move, searching for food. Longer casts and extended retrieves can make a considerable difference in saltwater fly fishing. Also, it is not easy to keep the fly deep enough in the water column. In many situations, just being able to swim the fly a few feet deeper can mean more hook-ups.

Another difficulty is that saltwater fly fishermen are confronted by the wind nearly all the time. There are very few saltwater fishing situations where God allows us to cast downwind; more often we have to throw into it. This is particularly true for anglers wading and fishing the surf, where a breeze blowing toward the land is standard.

Conventional weight-forward lines are fine for casting to 60 feet or so. But if repetitive casting to more than 70 feet is called for, it takes a strong and experienced fly fisherman to keep throwing that line for long. Also, the rear section of weight-forward lines is rather large in diameter, and this affects the angler's ability to shoot the fly to the distant target and also impedes the descent of the fly down into the water column on those occasions when he switches to a sinking line.

Tournament casters realized many years ago that if they attached extra-thin line behind the heavy forward portion at the front of the fly line, they could cast greater distances. Most fly fishermen refer to this line configuration, a heavy forward portion attached to an ultra-thin line, as a *shooting head* (though the manufacturers' designation is *shooting taper*). Thus, an 8-weight line with a 30-pound floating head attached to an ultra-thin shooting line is designated ST8F (Shooting Taper size 8 Floating). The ultra-thin line, generally referred to as *shooting line,* is simply a thin level line.

If you purchase a commercial shooting head, I suggest getting one a size larger than your rod calls for. Since you will always extend more than 30 feet of line outside the rod tip when you make a longer cast with a weight-forward line, a shooting head one size larger will load the rod better and allow you to shoot the line over a longer distance.

Line manufacturers sell a shooting line that is attached to the rear of a shooting head. This commercial line is nothing more than a level fly line that can vary in diameter and strength. Line strength can be as little as 12 pounds to more than 30 pounds. Shooting lines having a diameter less than .030 will probably test less than 20 pounds. *A shooting line that measures .035 or slightly larger is best for saltwater and big fishing situations, since smaller-diameter shooting lines are often weaker than the leader being used.* During a fight, if enough strain is put on the tackle handling a shooting line of .030 or smaller, the shooting line may break, causing you to lose the shooting head and the fish.

Fly fishermen use a variety of different materials for their shooting lines, including commercially manufactured shooting lines, monofilament (usually 30-pound test is preferred), and braided leader butt material. If you want to cast the greatest distance and fish the greatest depth using a shooting head, then monofilament is supreme. However, anglers who fish from the deck of a boat believe that monofilament is not ideal because the light line blows around too much in a breeze and tends to tangle.

Dan Blanton tipped me off to a great trick for handling this situation. If the deck is kept wet where the monofilament shooting line is lying, tangling problems are reduced. So now when I use mono shooting line, I carry a sponge and continually wet the deck where the mono is lying.

A braided leader butt line is okay, and it shoots exceptionally well. But it is very rough on the hands and can cut through the skin. Many anglers using this braided material tape their fingers to avoid cutting the skin.

Commercial shooting heads are generally 30 feet in length. But you can make your own head, one that casts farther than most commercial shooting heads. It's easy to do. Buy a double-taper line *one size larger than the rod calls for.* For example, if you are using a 9-weight rod, buy a 10-weight double-taper. Since the middle section of a double-taper line is level and tapers exactly the same way at each end, you can make two shooting heads from this line.

Measure back from one end of the double-taper and cut it off. Attach this head to a shooting line. If you are a good caster, capable of throwing 70 feet easily with a weight-forward line, then cut off 36 to 38 feet of the line. You will have a shooting head six to eight feet longer than a commercial 30-footer. Of course, since all fly lines fall to the water after they have unrolled or straightened at the end of the forward cast, your longer design will unroll a greater distance toward the target before it begins falling. If after practicing with this length you find it to be a length longer than you can comfortably handle, you can shorten it to a length you prefer.

If you have purchased a commercial shooting line, you will need to connect it to the back of the shooting head. Almost any fly shop sells a pair of braided loops for this purpose. One loop should be attached to the end of the shooting head and the other to the end of the shooting line. The two lines can then be looped together. *Whip-finish the ends of each loop.*

This loop-to-loop system gives you the advantage of always having a looped shooting line on the reel. You can then loop a variety of shooting heads onto the shooting line throughout the day to cope with changing fishing conditions. The disadvantage of the loop-to-loop system is that loops tend to run somewhat roughly through the fly rod guides.

Here is an alternate method to avoid that problem. Tease open the hollow ends of the shooting head and shooting line with a large needle. Then cut an angle on the back of the shooting line and the shooting head. Take about three inches of 30 to 50-pound braided butt leader material and carefully tease each tapered end of the shooting line into the hollow braided material. Once you have at least 1 1/2 inches of each fly line inserted into the braided line, trim any loose fuzz from the two braided line ends and either whip-finish the ends or glue just the frayed ends of the braided line to prevent them from unraveling. *Whip-finish or glue only the* ends *of the braided* material. *Allow the rest of the shooting head and shooting line to nestle inside the braided line.* Under tension, the braided line will act like a "Chinese finger" and clench the shooting head and shooting line together so tightly that they cannot be pulled off by even the strongest fish.

When you need to get your fly deep in the water column, a lead-core shooting head is ideal. This type of shooting head is made from lead-core trolling line and is preferably sheathed in braided plastic. Cut off the length of lead-core that you feel you can handle well. The shortest head I suggest is about 25 feet, the longest about 30 feet. The better you can cast, the longer the head you can use. Then attach this head to the shooting line. When you want to get as deep as possible, use monofilament as the shooting line. If depth is not quite as important, you'll have fewer problems with tangles on the cast if you use a conventional shooting line.

(For further details on shooting heads, lines, and their connections, you might want to refer to a companion volume in the Library, *Fly Fishing Knots and Connections,* pp. 89-101.)

Teeny Lines

The Teeny line is a specialty line that has won great acceptance among saltwater fly rodders who want to fish below the surface. This series of lines is actually a series of modified shooting heads that work wondrously well.

Unlike most sinking lines that taper to a thinner diameter at the front, the Teeny line is constructed so that the front of the line is a level sinking line. This means that all of the sinking portion of the line sinks at the same rate and the fly swims even with the line, not above it. To the rear of this sinking portion is a floating shooting line that flows through the rod guides better than a sinking line. The sinking portion of all Teeny lines is dark olive and the floating portion is a brighter color, making it easy for the fisherman to observe the point at which most or all of the sinking portion of the line has been retrieved from under the water so that he can initiate the pick-up for the back cast. The brighter colored portion of each line weight varies from weight to weight for easy identification.

A particular Teeny line is identified by a number which corresponds to the grains of weight in the sinking portion. Thus, a Teeny 300 has a front sinking portion that weighs 300 grains. It would cast well on a 7, 8, or 9-weight rod and is perhaps the most popular of all the Teeny lines. Every even-numbered line — i.e., 200, 300, 400, and 500 — has a total length of about 80 feet. The sinking heads of these lines are approximately 24 to 27 feet long.

In response to requests from many anglers who wanted longer sinking heads (which cast long distances very easily), Jim Teeny has now developed 100-foot lines with 30-foot sinking heads. These lines are numbered 350, 450, 550, and 650, figures that again correspond to the weight of the sinking portion in grains.

If you are considering fishing with sinking lines and want to get added distance without having to fool around with all types of connections, the Teeny lines are your answer.

Casting Sinking Lines and Heavy Flies

Until they know how to do it correctly, fly fishermen believe that casting a heavily weighted fly on a sinking line or lead-core shooting head should be avoided when possible. But once the problem is understood and dealt with, this type of casting is no longer burdensome or dangerous to the caster. In fact, such a rig can actually be easier to cast than a 5-weight floating line on a trout rod.

Using a Teeny 300 line for this discussion, in a typical situation before the back cast is begun the fisherman has placed

Steven Sawyer returning an albacore to the Atlantic. ➤

the line to his front, by means of either an earlier cast, a roll cast, or a false cast.

Keep in mind, first, that while a floating line during any cast tends to decrease in speed rather rapidly, a floating line with a heavily weighted fly on the leader, or a weighted line such as the Teeny 300, tends to travel on the back cast at a very high rate of speed; second, that for the most efficient back cast with a floating line, you want the line on the back cast to travel directly away from the target; and third, to begin the forward cast with a floating line, the line and fly must suddenly and very abruptly change direction. However, with the Teeny line or any other type of weighted rig, you do not want to execute such an abrupt change of direction. *For it is this abrupt change of direction that causes severe shock waves and the resulting tangles in the line and leader of a weighted line!*

In other words, the effective casting technique for heavily weighted and sinking lines needs to be *entirely different* from the technique you have always used with floating lines.

Once the fly fisherman understands that for these types of lines the solution is to avoid a quick change in direction at the end of the back cast, everything falls into place. Actually, fly casting a sinking line — even a lead-core shooting head — can be easier than throwing a floating line. The weight and speed of the line can be used to advantage once the angler learns how to eliminate that abrupt change in the direction of the cast.

Here's how to do it.

Make the cast to the rear as slowly as possible. And instead of the tight loop you normally make with a floating line, make a relatively wide loop at the end of the back cast. A tight loop traveling rapidly in one direction and then reversing in direction creates shock waves and tangles. A wide loop, on the other hand, causes the leader and fly to trail smoothly around a curve. The fly is then somewhat like a boat trailer attached to a car: as the car goes around a curve, the trailer follows smoothly behind. Once the leader and fly have rounded the curve and the line is moving toward the target, you can complete the motion of a normal forward cast. And a single haul will make everything go faster and farther.

The best way to execute this cast easily is to use a water haul, which is simply a variation of the roll cast. Here's the order of your casting motions:

1) Make a forward roll cast.

2) As the line and leader unroll in front of you, lower the rod toward the water. When the front end of the line unrolls and contacts the water, begin a low and gentle drawing back of the rod.

3) Make the slowest possible back cast that will carry the fly all the way to the rear. Don't try to make a rapid back cast! You also want the line to travel in a curving arc or well-rounded loop to the rear. Begin this back cast as if you were making a *low* side cast, with the hand low. The rod hand should travel to the rear in a "U" shape until the fly has been brought back and the forward cast is started. *This will require a* constant *pulling pressure on the rod throughout the back cast.*

Applying this constant, circular pressure throughout the back cast is often difficult for casters. There is a tendency to throw the line back straight as you would with a floating line. Here is a simple exercise to teach you how to apply the necessary constant pressure:

Extend about 12 feet of line outside the rod tip. Hold the rod parallel to the ground and at waist level. Rotate your wrist clockwise as if you were winding in line. Watch to make sure the line travels in a circle, not in an oval. If you were winding in line, the reel handle would travel in a perfect circle; try to make your forearm rotate the same way.

Now back to the cast. When you have the line swirling around in a circle, and your hand has rotated to the right and the rod tip is at the top of the circle . . .

4) Begin the forward cast. If you have been rotating your hand properly, you'll discover that the line drives well forward in the cast.

Try never to false cast sinking lines, weighted flies, or a leader with several items attached. False casting requires you to throw the line rather rapidly, entailing a quick change in direction at the end of each forward and back cast. If you make a water haul and a poor back cast results, don't false cast. Instead, make a gentle forward cast and drop the line to the surface in front of you. As soon as the line end falls to the surface, make another water haul.

When you have mastered the cast I have outlined in this section, you will be able to throw sinking lines, weighted flies, and even leaders with split-shot indicators and several flies attached — easily and free of tangles.

LEFTY'S SPECIAL WEEDGUARD

Weedguards come in many forms. The most popular are made with monofilament and are usually constructed in one of two ways: Either a prong of straight monofilament is attached so that it extends from the hook eye to just in front of the hook point; or a loop (sometimes a double loop) of monofilament is brought from the rear of the hook and secured in front. As I see it, the problem with monofilament weedguards is that they quickly become deformed. If the fly snags too often, the monofilament will eventually be bent out of shape from the fisherman pulling the fly loose. And after several fish have attacked the fly and chewed on the weedguard, the guard becomes mangled and almost useless.

Another popular type of weedguard, usually more durable than the monofilament guards, is made from stainless steel trolling wire. This guard is generally a straight piece of wire secured near the hook eye, which is slanted back to prevent the hook point from snagging up on weeds. Although it is better than the monofilament types, this guard has two disadvantages. The wire is very short, extending from behind the hook eye only to the hook point. When a fish strikes, it is difficult for this short lever to deflect so that the hook point engages in the fish. Also, if the wire is bent, it can become disconnected from the fly, leaving the fly guardless.

I have designed a weedguard that I believe is vastly superior to any existing weedguard, offering a number of advantages over other guards. One wonderful feature is that this weedguard can be added to most flies in your box without any modification to the fly. Another is that it collapses more easily on the strike, so it should provide you with better hookups. And this guard is actually a double guard, since it has two arms to protect the hook instead of one.

To make this weedguard, I generally use #5 (.014) solid stainless steel trolling wire, available in almost any shop that caters to saltwater fishermen. Some anglers prefer the slightly softer and more flexible #4 wire. In either dimension, you can use bright wire or what is often referred to as "coffee-colored" wire. Both work well.

As I mentioned, you can install the wire weedguard on an existing fly. However, if you are tying a fly from scratch (as the balance of these instructions will presume), leave about 1/8 inch of the hook shank bare immediately behind the hook eye. This will make it easier to secure the weedguard.

The length of wire you need to use is determined by the size and length of your hook. For most saltwater flies, 3 1/2 inches of wire should be okay. If you plan to make several weedguards of the same size, note down the length of wire you started with. When you clip the excess wire after installing your first weedguard, you'll have a better idea of the best length to cut for the next guard.

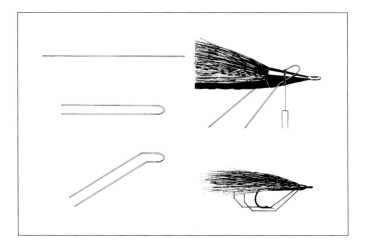

Lefty's Special Weedguard

Bend the wire at the middle to form a long and narrow horseshoe or "U" shape. Then, using a pair of pliers, bend the "U" shape at a 45-degree angle, about 1/8 inch back from curve of the "U." Now tie your fly. Secure the wire firmly to the hook shank and add a drop of glue for safety. Flex the two wire ends so that they slant back, and where they meet the hook point make a bend in the wires so that they lie parallel to the hook shank immediately behind the hook eye. Carefully bend the two wires one at a time so that they conform to the bend of the hook. Clip off any excess wire.

The final result is a double guard leading back from the hook eye, bent to protect the hook, the ends of the guard flowing into the wing of the fly.

This guard offers several advantages over other guards. A straight wire weedguard is short and doesn't collapse as easily. The straight guard also sometimes allows the leader to slip in behind the guard and spoil the cast. With my design, since the ends of the guards are hidden in the fly's wing, the chance of fouling the fly in the leader is reduced. And because the wires are bent to conform to the bend of the hook, a striking fish will tend to push the wire down, making it possible for the hook point to impale the fish. Best of all, if one wire of this double weedguard becomes too bent, it can be rocked back and forth and snapped free of the hook, leaving a single weedguard. One caution: should you have to remove one of the guards because it becomes deformed, never cut it off with pliers. This leaves a very sharp end on the wire, which can cut you. Instead, grasp the end of the wire and rock it back and forth until the wire breaks, leaving a smooth end.

While this written description may seem confusing, installing the guard is very simple. If you read the text and study the illustration, you'll find this is an easy guard to make.

USING CHUGGERS AND POPPING BUG/STREAMER COMBINATION RIGS TO TEASE FISH

Using a Chugger to Tease Fish

Every inshore fly fisherman should have a plug casting or spinning rod in his fishing arsenal, not to be used to catch fish but to excite and stimulate fish into striking a presented fly. One other item is necessary — a chugger, which is simply a surface lure that *carries no hooks* and is constructed with a cupped face. It should be of a size and weight to attract the fish you want to catch. Usually, the ideal chugger has a cupped face and is about three inches long and 3/4 inch to one inch in diameter.

The chugger is a valuable tool because many inshore fish won't respond readily to a streamer fly that swims silently through the water. Others will take a look at a streamer but won't attack it because they are not very excited. The chugger can often provoke the fish into hitting your offering.

To use the chugger, have your guide or companion cast it (with the plug or spinning rod) into an area where fish are likely to be holding, while you have your line ready to cast. When your companion flips the rod tip quickly, the chugger will make a loud "blooping" sound. By retrieving line and frequently flipping the rod tip, he can make the chugger dance on the surface and create a constant series of loud blooping sounds. This furious surface activity causes many species of fish to attack. As a fish makes attempts to eat the dancing lure, your companion should continue to draw the chugger closer to the boat. Usually the fish will grab the wooden or plastic lure several times, and because the fish is so excited, it won't notice the lure is not naturally soft or yielding.

When the fish is within casting range, present your fly as close to the chugger as possible. If the chugger is stopped dead in the water and the fly swims close by, the fish will tend to attack the fly immediately. If this doesn't happen, make another cast.

Let me cite several examples of how a chugger can work for you.

Ladyfish are particularly excited by a small chugger worked across the surface. A big ladyfish weighs only two or three pounds, so a smaller chugger works best, and a streamer fly of about two inches will almost always draw a strike after the fish is excited.

Cobia will frequently ignore a streamer, since these larger fish prefer a very big fly. However, if you toss a big chugger to a cobia, it will turn the fish on like nothing you ever saw. Once the cobia is really worked up, it will take the streamer fly it would otherwise normally refuse.

A chugger is also helpful when there is a slack tide around a channel marker or buoy. Cobia, snook, tripletail, jewfish, and other species often lie deep beneath the marker or buoy. A chugger can pull the fish to the surface where the fly fisherman can get a shot at them. Chuggers can be used to lure fish away from markers and buoys, too. Since markers are encrusted with line-cutting barnacles and buoys are anchored by chains that hold these same creatures, it is best to lure the fish away from these areas before making the cast.

Throwing a chugger at a school of jack crevalle is like rolling a wine bottle into a jail cell. And while bluefish are sometimes reluctant to take a fly, a chugger will frequently excite them into hitting almost any fly pattern you toss them after the chugger has done its job. Chuggers will also work on striped bass that have been refusing your flies. Saltwater fly fishermen should remember that chuggers can be used in many different situations to persuade reluctant fish to strike.

How to Make a Chugger

While you can buy chuggers in some outlets, it may be easier to make your own. Making a chugger is a simple operation. Get a wooden dowel about 3/4 inch to one inch in diameter and about 2 1/2 to three inches in length. Use a grinding tool to make a depressed cup in the face of the lure. About 3/4 inch behind the cup, taper the lure so that the back end is smaller than the front. Add a stout screw eye to the center of the cupped area; this is where you will attach the plug or spinning line. At the rear of the chugger, attach another screw eye, and to the eye, attach a 1/8 or 1/4-ounce sinker. The sinker will make the rear of the chugger dip downward when it is motionless on the surface of the water so that the chugger will not have the appearance of a conventional casting plug; but the added weight will assist you in casting the chugger and creating noise on the retrieve.

If you feel that making a chugger is too much trouble, you can buy a similar surface lure from many bass-fishing tackle stores and adapt it for teasing fish. Simply remove the hooks and add a sinker to the rear screw eye.

How to Make a Popping Bug/Streamer Combination Rig

Another deadly method of catching a number of inshore species by teasing them is through the use of a popping bug in combination with a streamer. After I give you directions for making this rig, I'll explain how to use it when fishing.

Select a popping bug, preferably one with a tail of bucktail rather than feathers, since a feather tail does seem to cause tangling. The bug should be small enough to be easy to cast, but it shouldn't be too large. Since a streamer fly is often tied to the bug, the popper should be big enough to support the streamer and not sink below the surface.

While many streamer flies can be used, I favor the Clouser Minnow. The weighted eyes on this pattern tend to flip over better at the end of the cast, resulting in less tangling, and they also cause the fly to sink well below the popping bug during the retrieve. In most cases, a Clouser Minnow about two to three inches long is ideal. A bit of Mylar flash material such as Flashabou or Crystal Flash helps draw strikes.

Use a length of 12 to 20-pound monofilament, a length that measures six to 10 inches after the bug is connected to the streamer fly; a longer strand will usually tangle. Tie one end of the monofilament to the streamer fly, and attach the other end of the monofilament to the popping bug by tying an Improved Clinch Knot onto the hook of the bug just above the barb. But I find a better connection is a Nail Knot, as it will secure the monofilament on the straight part of the hook shank just behind the bug's body. (For instructions on tying these knots, see a companion volume in the Library, *Fly Fishing Knots and Connections.*)

How to Use a Popping Bug/Streamer Combination Rig

Once you have the bug and streamer fly rigged, cast them where you think fish may be holding and then begin a retrieve that you would use with any popper. The bug will gurgle and make popping sounds, attracting certain fish. When a fish reaches the bug, it will then see the dangling, dancing streamer and will usually be enticed into striking. Sometimes the fish will take the bug, but most often it will hit the streamer fly.

Three fish very receptive to this rig are spotted seatrout, weakfish, and striped bass up to about 12 pounds. All of these fish cruise waters that are often 5 to 10 feet deep, and a silent, retrieved streamer may be missed or ignored by the fish down below. However, the popper's noise will draw them to the surface and get you your strike. I find that for striped bass, a streamer or Clouser Minnow representing baitfish is often the best producer. For seatrout and weakfish, use a streamer fly or Clouser Minnow with a lot of color.

OVERLEAF: *A selection of striper flies and tackle.*

CHAPTER FOUR

THE NINE ESSENTIAL INSHORE SALTWATER PATTERNS

Most of us are aware of how complex the selection of fly patterns for freshwater fishing — particularly trout fishing — has become over the years. Today, it's easy to understand why people new to fly fishing can be led to believe they will have to master Latin, learn a whole new intricate vocabulary, and memorize the names and characteristics of dozens of patterns in order to become proficient freshwater anglers. A knowledge of all of these things may make the sport more interesting, but it certainly isn't necessary to catch trout.

This same trend of complexity seems to be creeping into saltwater fly fishing. It can be fun to learn all about the creatures that crawl around the bottom or swim in saltwater; I am not knocking anyone getting seriously involved in saltwater who wants to master all aspects of the game. But saltwater fly fishing is not necessarily complicated, certainly not when it comes to selecting the flies you will need.

For inshore saltwater fly fishing, I recommend that you start with a bare-bones selection of nine particular fly patterns, patterns that will bring you success most of the time, almost anywhere you fish. Of course, from time to time you may want to vary size, length, and color of these patterns to suit your individual preferences or special fishing situations, but with these flies you should be well prepared for every inshore salt-water fly fishing species you encounter — striped bass, red-fish, snook, barramundi, bluefish, snapper, threadfin salmon, jack crevalle, dogtooth tuna, albacore, shark, barracuda — need I go on? Many of these patterns can also serve double duty for use on various offshore bluewater fish, such as am-berjack, yellowfin tuna, dolphin, cobia, or mackerel; even triple duty for fishing to the three famed flats' species, bone-fish, permit, and tarpon.

With these nine patterns, you will be able to fish with all types and configurations of floating and sinking lines, in all types of inshore waters — on coral and sand flats, in weed-filled bays, in mangrove lagoons, in the surf — and at all water depths — on the surface to way down deep.

You will see that after a brief discussion of six patterns — the popping bug, the crab fly, Surf Candy, Sar-Mul-Mac, Whistler, and Seaducer — I will be giving even more detailed information on the Big Three of the group, the three patterns I just wouldn't dream of going to saltwater without. These indispensable flies are the Clouser Minnow, the Bend Back, and the Lefty's Deceiver. After more than 50 years of fishing in both fresh and saltwater, I have concluded that the two best underwater flies today are the Clouser Minnow and the Lefty's Deceiver. And for fishing in places where your fly may snag frequently on the retrieve, I long ago added the Bend Back to my list of essential patterns.

POPPING BUG

The popping bug is an essential fly for many reasons. While a streamer is a silent offering, a popper attracts attention by its noise. It resembles prey that is helpless and unable to es-

Standard Popping Bug

cape — something few predatory fish can ignore. A popper can draw strikes from larger fish and also from fish that might not otherwise notice a conventional fly. One principal reason for the pattern's effectiveness is that a large popping bug creates an illusion of something much larger. Larger cobia and amberjack rarely take a streamer fly; they want something big, and often a popper will do the trick.

CRAB FLY

Crabs can be found in every sea and represent a substantial meal to most predatory fish. They are one of the finest natural baits for permit, tarpon, and striped bass, but you don't need to fish exact imitations of local crabs. I have had great success using just one crab design, Del Brown's Permit Fly,

Del Brown's Permit Fly

tied in various color combinations that match those of the crabs in the area I am fishing. When saltwater fishing, you should arm yourself with some "eyeless" crab flies that float, other crab patterns with lightweight eyes that sink slowly, and still others with heavy eyes that will sink quickly. Most of the time, the best presentation is simply to let the crab dead-drift with the tide. Few fly rodders realize just how effective this fly can be on many types of fish in all saltwaters.

SURF CANDY

This terrific fly is generally tied in small sizes. It normally should not exceed four inches in length. It is one of the best

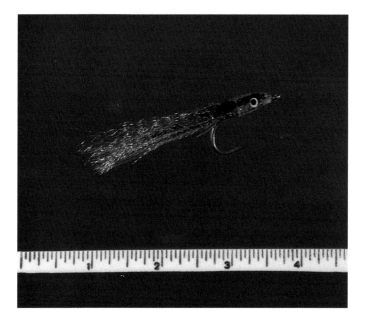

Surf Candy

imitations of small local baitfish that I have ever come across. Additionally it casts beautifully and is very durable. The original Surf Candy had a coating of epoxy over the hook shank area of the fly pattern. But Bob Popovics, who developed the fly, now uses clear bathroom silicone sealer instead of epoxy. The body of this newer Surf Candy looks the same, but the silicone is softer, and better hook-ups occur when the fish strike.

SAR-MUL-MAC

Dan Blanton's Sar-Mul-Mac is a great fly for imitating various baitfish. Like the Lefty's Deceiver and the Clouser Minnow described below, it is tied in different color combinations to

Sar-Mul-Mac

match local species. It is nearly always tied weighted, which I believe improves fishing success.

WHISTLER

This fly, also originated by Dan Blanton, is another superior pattern for many saltwater species. It is one of the best flies for fishing deep or in dirty water. Its bulky head and large

Whistler

bead-chain eyes "push" water, which sets up sound vibrations that help fish locate the fly. The original pattern was tied very bulky and with some weight, usually lead wire added to the hook shank. But Dan also ties it to swim high in the water column. The Whistler has produced for me in many waters.

SEADUCER

The Seaducer is a very old pattern, dating back to the last century. It was first developed as a bass fly. Unlike most patterns, it sinks so slowly in the water column that it appears suspended. The palmered hackles at the front and the long, fluffy hackles forming the tail or wing act like outriggers, so that the fly can be fished slowly in just inches of water without snagging bottom. The hook shank is wound its full length

Seaducer

with as many saddle hackles as can be tied there. The whole thing ends up resembling a multi-legged caterpillar with a supple saddle-hackle tail. The fly lands on the surface of the water like a thistle, so it can be dropped close to wary fish without frightening them. The pattern can be tied short or long, and in a variety of color combinations.

CLOUSER MINNOW

Every saltwater angler should carry this essential fly. Originally developed for smallmouth bass, the pattern has a host of variations and ranges in length from one inch to one foot. At this writing, I have caught 79 species of fish around the world in fresh and saltwater on this fly. The fly has deceived 40-pound narrow-barred mackerel (Tanguique) off the north coast of New Zealand, threadfin salmon on Bathurst Island in Australia, giant trevally at Christmas Island, Niugini black bass in the salty river mouths of New Guinea, barracuda in the Bahamas, dolphin off the South American coast, sailfish in the Pacific waters off Costa Rica, and snook, bonefish, permit, tarpon, and redfish in the Bahamas and Florida.

As I discussed in my bonefish book, this fly is absolute dynamite on bonefish. Let me tell you how good it is. Several years ago, my best friend, Irv Swope, and I were fishing at the Andros Island Bonefish Club in the Bahamas with Rupert Leadon, who owns the lodge. One day, on the west side of Andros, we landed 36 bonefish of an average weight of more than 6 pounds each — four weighing more than 10 pounds, and one topping 11 pounds. The largest fish were weighed on an accurate scale. *Every fish was caught on a Clouser Minnow* dressed on a #2 hook with a wing about 2 1/2 inches long, consisting of a white underwing, a good bit of pearl Crystal Flash over that, and a top wing of chartreuse.

Two Examples of the Clouser Minnow

If I had to choose just two patterns to fly fish for bonefish for the rest of my life, I would select the white/chartreuse Clouser described above, along with a color variation achieved by changing the top wing from chartreuse to light tan. Using these two Clouser Minnow patterns in a variety of hook sizes, I have been able to catch bonefish wherever I have found them, from the South Pacific to the Florida Keys.

So what is this Clouser Minnow pattern, and what makes it so effective?

Bob Clouser, who runs a fly shop in Middletown, Pennsylvania, conceived the original fly. Bob wanted something that resembled a minnow that smallmouth bass would hit. The first one he handed to me brought on the same reaction I get from many fly fishermen when they see it for the first time: it looks like an unfinished fly, and it appears not to have enough dressing. But the secret to the effectiveness of this fly,

I think, is that, more than any other pattern I have ever fished with, it is an absolutely superb imitation of many fresh and saltwater baitfish. When you look at a minnow or baitfish in the water, you don't really notice caudal fins, gill covers, or other details. Instead, you see what is the "suggestion" of a baitfish — a partial or indistinct body and often an eye. The Clouser Minnow is designed to imitate just these character-istics, and when retrieved, it closely resembles a minnow.

The pattern has another asset: it gets down — and fast! In fairly deep-water fishing, and when fish show up near the boat, one of the problems with many fly patterns is that the fly doesn't sink quickly enough. The buoyant materials in most patterns keep them near the surface rather than down with the fish. A Clouser Minnow tied with FisHair or Ultra Hair and heavy lead eyes will go down like an anvil in a swamp. And since the eyes are attached on top of the hook and the wing is tied in reverse, the hook point rides up instead of down. This allows the fly to be fished over many types of bottom with little chance of snagging.

The Clouser Minnow is not an exact combination of col-ors and materials. Like the Lefty's Deceiver, it is a fly design. The original Clouser Minnow was tied on a #2 hook, with a wisp of bucktail dressing. Since then, hook size and the color and length of the wing have varied widely. The fly can be as short as 1/2 inch or as long as 12 inches. It can have a wing of whatever materials and colors you choose.

The eyes can be of bead chain or lead or other metallic materials and can vary in weight. The fly is always tied with weighted eyes at the front. Nearly all the successful patterns are tied with lead eyes, available at many fly shops. For most flats fishing, these sizes of eyes are the most popular: 5/32 inch (1/50 ounce); 3/16 inch (1/36 ounce); and 7/32 inch (1/24

Striper fishermen enjoying a beautiful sunset. ➤

ounce). For deeper water fishing in channels and on the open sea, the two largest lead eye sizes are frequently used: 1/4 inch (1/18 ounce) and 9/32 inch (1/10 ounce).

By changing the weight of the metallic eyes, the length of the wing, the size of the hook, and the combination of colors of the basic Clouser Minnow pattern, this can be a productive pattern on a wide range of saltwater species.

Tying the Clouser Minnow

To match a Clouser Minnow to your own special fishing needs, determine what kind of baitfish is being fed on by the species you seek, then tie a Clouser in that color and length. For some baitfish, such as alewives and pilchards (which have a rather deep belly), you should tie the Clouser a little fuller than usual.

If you are trying to imitate baitfish that have a medium brown body about 2 1/2 inches long and a lighter tan belly, tie the fly this way: Place a hook in the vise, and attach a pair of 1/36-ounce or 1/24-ounce lead eyes to the shank, approxi-

Clouser Minnow With and Without Lefty's Special Weedguard

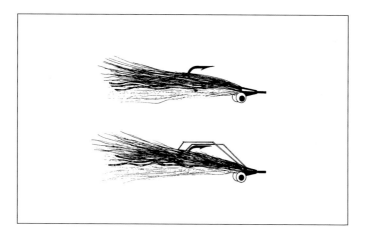

mately 1/4 inch behind the hook eye. Turn the hook over in the vise so that the shank is down and the point is up. Directly in front of the lead eyes, tie in some light tan bucktail about the length of your little finger. *Don't overdress the fly.* On top of the bucktail, tie in about a half dozen copper strands of Crystal Flash or Flashabou. On top of that, tie in dark brown bucktail in the same amount as the light tan. When finished, the entire fly should appear sparsely tied.

That's all there is to it! If the fly is to be fished in heavy grass or over a rocky bottom, I recommend tying in a wire weedguard before attaching the lead eyes.

To make a Clouser for imitating larger open-water baitfish, tie a heavy pair of lead eyes (1/18 or 1/10 ounce) on a #4/0 hook. Since bucktail is fairly short, tie the wing portion in Ultra Hair or a similar long, synthetic hair used in streamer flies. Then tie in some long (five to 10 inches), white Ultra Hair for the belly, and above that attach some pearl Crystal Flash. Finally, use a little green or blue Ultra Hair for the top wing, as many baitfish in the open water are white on the belly and green or blue on the back.

BEND BACK

This is another pattern developed decades ago for bass fishing in the mid South. In the Bend Back fly, the hook shank is slightly bent and the wing is tied reverse-style so that the hook point rides up instead of down when retrieved.

As far as I can tell, the Bend Back was first used before the turn of the century. Bass fishermen in the mid South were plagued by dense thickets of lily pads and other aquatic vegetation where largemouth bass roamed. Conventional patterns didn't work well because the hook point hanging down snagged too often. A reverse-tied fly with a bent hook was

Bend Back

the answer because it could be cast up on weeds sticking above the surface, dragged across them, and dropped into the open pockets where bass were not used to seeing a fly.

Since the late 1960s, the Bend Back fly has really gained popularity, especially in saltwater. Because the hook rides up, I find that it is very effective on just about all species but larger tarpon. The roof of a larger tarpon's mouth is like hard, smooth plastic, for it is mostly bone. I have missed many strikes on larger tarpon with the Bend Back, so I no longer use it for them.

One of the best places to use a Bend Back is along a mangrove shoreline, where you're casting to snook, redfish, snappers, and other fish lurking among the spider-leg roots that are ready to snag your fly. You can also use the Bend Back when you want to cast tight against the bank; conventionally tied flies mean serious hook-up problems. And the Bend Back is ideal for swimming around docks or rotten underwater pilings, where many species, including striped bass, are to be found. You can fish the pattern with little fear of hanging up.

In the mid-Atlantic area there are times when stripers are holding close to the bottom over oyster bars. Oyster shells are famous for snagging the hook. A Bend Back, however, can be crawled over the bottom, right in front of the nose of a striped bass. If you are considering using the Bend Back for this kind of fishing and you tie a body material on the hook shank, I suggest you coat the bottom of the streamer body with five-minute epoxy. This gives the fly a protective shield against the sharp edges of the oyster shells.

There are many other places where the Bend Back comes in handy. Bar jacks, dolphin, blue runners, rainbow runners, cobia, and many other predatory species feed among the sargassum weedlines offshore, since these are some of the few places small fish can hide in the open sea. Sargassum and loose bay grass can frustrate the fly fisherman because they tend to shuttle down the line and snag the fly. You need a weedless fly for fishing in grass, and while weedguards work fairly well, the Bend Back is much more effective.

In the Northeast, anglers fishing inshore are also plagued by floating grass. These fishermen either wade the surf, where grass collects after being brought into shore by the waves, or fish from boats close to shore. Striper fishermen who work the waters at night often don't realize that their fly has fouled from weeds. Few fish ever strike a fly with weeds dangling from it. A Bend Back used at night insures a snag-free retrieve.

My favorite form of fly fishing is fishing for bonefish. In dense beds of turtle grass, which are prime feeding locations for bonefish, popular bonefish flies such as the Clouser Minnow and the Crazy Charley are difficult to fish. But where patterns with metallic eyes like the ones on these flies will constantly hang up, a Bend Back can be drawn through the thick stands of turtle grass with little chance of snagging. I also use the Bend Back on bonefish cruising a very shallow flat covered in fly-catching coral. The Bend Back is by far the best pattern for this situation.

I fish the Bend Back to great advantage along a steep bank that is rather free of debris and that drops rapidly into deeper water. Using a fast-sinking line and a long leader (at least 12 feet), I cast the fly and most of the leader up on the bank. I let the sinking line reach the bottom in the deeper water and then I begin a slow retrieve. The leader and line will crawl across the bank and enter the water. I continue the slow retrieve so that the leader drags the fly down along the side of the steep bank and follows the path of the sinking line, which is lying on the bottom. Many times, a fish seeing a fly crawling down the bank underwater and then across the bottom can't resist — and a strike follows.

Another situation in which I enjoy using a Bend Back is when snook, barramundi, redfish, threadfin salmon, snappers, or other species are lying under an overhanging branch and are very spooky. If a fly is dropped into the water at the end of the cast, the splash will often frighten the fish. With a Bend Back streamer, I can deliberately throw the fly into the branches above the fish. If I jerk on the line, the hook may snag, but if I tease the line slowly, the Bend Back will almost always crawl over the branches and drop into the water with a gentle splash. I've seen several snook and one nice barramundi watch the fly crawling through the branches and then grab it when it fell to the surface.

Tying the Bend Back

The Bend Back is an easy fly to tie, but there are a few simple rules to follow that make it effective. If the wing is tied too sparsely, the fly may not travel with the hook-up. So you need a moderately full and buoyant wing to keep it riding properly on the retrieve. Because bucktail is buoyant, it is the preferred wing material for Bend Backs. The biggest mistake is to bend the hook too much before tying the pattern. If too great a bend is made, the hook shank dangles below the wing and strikes are often refused. *The wing and body of a properly tied Bend Back will swim as a unit when retrieved.*

To tie the Bend Back, clamp the hook upside down (point up) in the vise, and using pliers, grip the hook just behind the eye — 1/8 to 3/8 inch back, depending on the size of the hook. Start bending the hook downward. The instant you feel the hook just begin to bend, stop! You can dress the shank as you would that of any standard streamer. I tie the wing only on that portion of the hook that I did not bend. *I have stopped putting any other material on the hook shank besides the wing material. A bare shank causes the fly to ride with the hook point up. The body material that is usually tied on a Bend Back will often wear away when the fly is dragged on the bottom.*

That's it. Like the Clouser Minnow and Lefty's Deceiver, the Bend Back is a style of tying a fly, rather than an exact pattern. You can tie the Bend Back on hooks as small as #6 for bonefish and as large as a #5/0 for offshore fishing. You can also tie a popping bug Bend Back-style.

LEFTY'S DECEIVER

I began developing this pattern in the late 1950s. Around 1958, I was living in Maryland and fishing in Chesapeake Bay for striped bass, which we called rockfish. A constant companion in those days was Tom Cofield, outdoor editor of the *Baltimore News-American*. Much of our fishing was in the lower bay around Crisfield, Maryland. At least in our area, few people aside from the writer, Joe Brooks, bothered to go after stripers with a fly. But Tom and I enjoyed this great fishing.

Several Examples of the Lefty's Deceiver

However, all was not sweet. The flies used in those days were rather crude compared to today's wonderful modern creations. The body usually consisted of chenille with a feather or bucktail wing. Many retrieves were spoiled because the wing would foul or under-wrap the hook on the cast. These patterns were often difficult to throw because of the air resistance built into them.

On a trip home Tom and I discussed what would be the desirable features of a good fly for saltwater work. We determined it should have a baitfish shape, shouldn't foul, and should be easy to cast — even at long distances in a breeze. It should have a good swimming action, and, of course, it should appeal to the fish. It was this experience and discussion that gave rise to the Lefty's Deceiver.

My first version of the pattern was a simple all-white fly, with just a feather wing and a bucktail collar. It was about four inches long and was tied to imitate alewives, the baitfish

A Lefty's Deceiver Showing the Same Fly in Different Lengths

so prevalent in the shallows of the Chesapeake. This was before the days of Mylar and the fancy plastic reflective products now incorporated into flies. But as simple as this pattern was, it sure worked.

A little later, I began to modify the color combinations, adding a little red at the throat to imitate gills and attaching some peacock herl to the top. I also started tying the fly in various lengths to match different baitfish.

In the early 1960s, I wrote about the pattern and suggested others try it. For some time there was little feedback, but gradually people began using the fly. Today, many patterns bearing other names are simply modifications of the Lefty's Deceiver. Under whatever name, perhaps more saltwater fish have been caught on the Lefty's Deceiver pattern than on any other fly. In fact, it may currently be the most popular saltwater fly in the world. And surprisingly, it's a very effective pattern for fishing freshwater, as well.

Tying the Lefty's Deceiver

Too many people fail to realize that this fly can be tied in many ways and for different fishing purposes. There are many variations of the pattern. The Lefty's Deceiver is not really a strict pattern but rather, like the Clouser and the Bend Back, a style or method of tying a fly. It can have a slightly different shape and be tied in many colors and lengths. The fly can be tied as short as two inches and longer than a foot for billfish, amberjack, and other species. It can be tied in a Bend Back fashion or with the hook reversed. In its many forms, it has caught everything from striped bass to barramundi, tarpon, seatrout, mackerel, wahoo, bluefish, and billfish.

The basic method is to tie in a wing at the rear of the hook, carry the thread forward, and build a collar around the hook shank just behind the eye. *The tip ends of the collar must flow well behind the hook bend to help prevent the wing from underwrapping and to give the body its fishlike shape.* When I tie the fly to imitate a baitfish, I like to add a throat of either red Flashabou or red Crystal Flash. I think fish perceive this red area of the pattern as gills.

To receive full benefit from the Lefty's Deceiver, you need to analyze what you are trying to do and match the type of fly to the existing fishing conditions. The following are suggestions for tying the fly to suit various fishing situations.

Since the fly is most often used to imitate baitfish, I recommend you take the time to determine the size and shape of the bait in your area. Many times, dead baitfish collect around docks and boat ramps; examining the stomach contents of one of these fish can often be revealing. Talking to tackle shop owners and other fishermen may also give you a clue about the baitfish. Perhaps the best of all Lefty's Deceivers is still the all-white pattern, but if your local baitfish have a dark green back, then adding a little dark green bucktail or synthetic hair to the top of the fly will often increase strikes.

Where sand eels are prevalent and being fed on avidly by predatory fish, as in New England waters, a very sleek fly is called for. Dean Clark of Shrewsbury, Massachusetts, has been fishing for striped bass for years using variations of the Lefty's Deceiver. His sand eel imitation is simple and effective. It's a Lefty's Deceiver dressed on a #2 hook, with just two thin, white saddle hackles no more than 3 1/2 inches long tied at the rear. The body is white thread wrapped the full length of the hook. At the front, perhaps 20 fibers of white bucktail are tied on the sides and bottom, with a topping of no more than a dozen strands of olive bucktail. Dean uses very small Mylar eyes, which are glued to either side at the head. A coat of clear head cement on the head completes the pattern. The fly in the water looks very, very sleek — exactly like a sand eel.

To show how you might vary the Deceiver, even in the same region, let's look at how Brock Apfel of South Harpswell, Maine, often ties his flies for fishing for striped bass in big, deep rivers near his home. Using a #2/0 or #3/0 standard-length hook, he ties in about a dozen saddle hackles (yellow, white, or other color combinations) at the rear. He attaches them to the hook by lashing the stubs along the shank, which helps to build bulk along the body of the fly. The hook shank is then wrapped from the back to within 1/2 inch of the front with lead fuse wire. Then a full collar of heavily tied bucktail encircles the hook, with the tips of the bucktail flowing well behind the bend. In front of the collar he may tie in a pair of heavy lead eyes, 1/24 to 1/10 ounce, depending on how deep the fly is to be fished. Finally, the head is built up with thread and then coated with cement.

The two flies cited here, Dean Clark's and Brock Apfel's, are both fished for striped bass in the same region. But they look entirely different. The sand eel is so sleek it can barely be seen in the water. Brock's fly is weighted so heavily that it drops like a bomb as soon as it contacts the surface, and the bulky underbody and dense wing make it very visible. I'm sure the fly's bulk must set up some attractive sound waves, too, while it is retrieved through the water column.

The Lefty's Deceiver can be tied to be very effective on predatory fish feeding on bait trapped by waves crashing against rocky shorelines. Knowledgeable fly fishermen take many striped bass in these areas along the northeast coast of the United States. To tie this version of the Deceiver, make the rear of the fly as you would a normal pattern, using six to eight saddle hackles. But make the collar as bulky as you can from bucktail.

The collar on a Lefty's Deceiver is nearly always constructed of bucktail, which is a buoyant material. By decreasing or increasing the amount of bucktail in the collar, the pattern can be dressed so that it sinks rather quickly or almost suspends in the water. A bulky collar will cause the fly to suspend or sink very slowly.

Cast the fly right into the foam crashing and washing among the rocks and allow the fly to wash around. If you put enough bucktail in the collar, the fly will seem to stripers like a confused baitfish that has been swept into this hostile area and is trying to get out.

Not all Lefty's Deceivers imitate baitfish. Some are tied in bright colors. One of the best attractor types is a white-and-chartreuse combination. It has worked for me around most of the world. And a favorite of many experienced anglers is an all-black pattern. I favor black with a dash of either dark blue or purple Flashabou or Crystal Flash. The first time I fished the Northern Territory of Australia I was amazed to find that the overwhelming choice by fly fishermen there was a full-dressed, black Lefty's Deceiver. The flats in that region have six to nine-foot tides, which means many areas contain slightly roiled or dirty water. The fish seem to be able to locate this black fly better than other patterns.

The Lefty's Deceiver is one of my favorite patterns for tarpon. I can't tell you how many tarpon have been fooled by it. Big tarpon sometimes ignore small flies, all the rage today. In the spring in the Florida Keys, the average big tarpon must look at several dozen Keys-style tarpon flies a day. Sometimes a four to six-inch Lefty's Deceiver tied to represent a baitfish and undulated slowly in front of a giant tarpon is just the ticket. In fact, one of the three most popular of all tarpon flies is the Cockroach, which is simply a variation of the Deceiver.

Another example of the pattern adjusted and tied to suit local conditions is the Glades Deceiver pattern. When you're casting flies among the hook-grabbing mangrove roots of the saltwater section of the Everglades, you need a pattern that doesn't snag in the roots easily but appeals to the fish. Like the various Bend Back patterns, the Glades Deceiver was developed for this situation. But it is a good inshore pattern in many other places as well. This Deceiver is tied with a short 2 1/2 to 3-inch wing, a red throat, a calftail collar, and a #5 stainless steel trolling-wire weedguard.

Dean Clark, tyer of the sand eel imitation, is typical of good fishermen exploiting the pattern to catch fish in their particular area. In a telephone conversation, I asked Dean to send me samples of what he ties. I received nine Lefty's Deceivers — all different and for purposes as varied as surface fishing to seeking striped bass at night.

OVERLEAF: *Mark Lewchik enjoys a successful day of striped bass fishing off the coast of Martha's Vineyard.*

CHAPTER FIVE

FISHING FOR
STRIPED BASS

The striped bass is currently the most popular saltwater species being sought with a fly rod in most of the United States
(excluding the Gulf Coast and Florida). West Coast striped
bass fishing has declined in the past decade or so, but it is
still good in places such as the delta area near San Francisco
Bay. Our Atlantic Coast fishery was in serious trouble during
the 1980s, only turning around when the federal government
stepped in and forced the states to take action to save the fishery by declaring a complete moratorium on fishing for stripers along the mid-Atlantic Coast. This is another wonderful
example of how wise environmental controls, including the
restriction of fish harvesting for specified periods of time, can
create a marked improvement in the quality of our sport fishing. Today, striped bass range from Maine to South Carolina
in numbers recently unheard of.

But further declines in our Atlantic Coast striper population are possible, so the crisis is far from over. Scientists still
don't really know why there are good and bad years of striper
reproduction. Until they do, we should be careful about al-
lowing heavy harvesting by either sport or commercial fishermen. The striped bass now living on our Atlantic and Pacific
coasts make up our seed stock, and until we determine why
stripers reproduce abundantly and we take the steps neces-

sary to foster that reproduction, we need to enforce intelligent conservation measures to preserve the fish we have.

Most saltwater fly fishermen coming into the game now are fishing for striped bass. While there were relatively few striper fly fishers in the 1950s through the 1970s, the angling population has increased dramatically since the species made its comeback. From Virginia to New England (especially New England), thousands of anglers are now catching stripers on fly rods. We are catching them day and night, from the beach, from the rocks, and from boats. We know that striper behavior varies from place to place, and we have learned how to modify our fishing technique to fly fish for stripers in the various areas of their habitat. Meanwhile, we have witnessed tremendous improvement in striper fly-fishing tackle and flies.

WHERE, WHEN, AND HOW TO FISH FOR STRIPERS

Before going into detail on how to rig for and catch striped bass on the fly, let me outline a few basic points about the species. Stripers are basically inshore fish. Unlike tuna and other ocean roamers, they are rarely found more than a few miles from land. Even during migrations they tend to stay near the coastal shorelines.

I have limited experience with striped bass fishing on the West Coast. But one of my principal home waters, Chesapeake Bay, is regarded as the primary nursery ground for stripers on the East Coast, and I have spent a day or two on that water, you may be sure! The Hudson River and some other river systems also contribute to the stock of our Atlantic Coast striper population, but the Chesapeake is the main source.

Since spawning generally takes place in this area, stripers that have been ranging along the coast north of Maryland all the way to Maine must return to the Chesapeake. While stripers often overwinter in the Chesapeake, it is believed that many of these larger bass also hold off the mouth of the Chesapeake in the Atlantic Ocean.

Spawning takes place in very early spring in the major river systems of the Chesapeake Bay. Timing of the event depends on the water temperature of the spawning grounds. By late March, a slow migration begins out of the Chesapeake. Stripers either travel south and out the mouth of the bay or else swim through the ship canal at the northern extreme end of the Chesapeake and on into Delaware Bay.

A trigger for migration of striped bass is the movement of baitfish. These fish begin appearing along the coast as far north as Maine by early May, sometimes earlier. The baitfish generally enter the estuaries and rivers early; by late June, many have moved to the coast and even a little offshore. This means that by mid July, fishermen will find that many of the larger striped bass have left the rivers and shallow bays and are feeding a mile or so from the coast. However, stripers will move to the beaches and into rivers after darkness. Therefore, dusk and dawn in the summer often offer the best opportunities for catching a big striped bass.

Fly fisherman tend to rush the season and start casting in April or earlier in hopes of catching stripers as they move northward. But rarely is there any good fly fishing in the Chesapeake Bay before early or mid May. This is also the case in New Jersey. Off Long Island and even further north in Rhode Island and Massachusetts, an occasional striped bass is taken in early May, but the real fishing doesn't begin until mid to late May, when the first of smaller fish (commonly referred to as "schoolies") arrive. The bigger stripers are usually two to three weeks behind the smaller, earliest stripers in northern waters. In early May, along the shore of Long Island and further north there often appear huge schools of two to three-inch sand eels. Daytime fishing can be difficult because the stripers are feeding offshore, but at dusk and dawn, fly fishermen using small imitations of this bait can have some great catches along the beach.

Very early in the season, the rivers and estuaries are generally more productive than along the coast. One reason for this is that the baitfish seem to choke the rivers and estuaries at this time. Another reason is that the estuaries and many shallow rivers have dark mud bottoms. *A dark bottom in clear shallow water soaks up the sun's heat. Waters in these areas can be five to seven degrees warmer than in coastal areas, and fish are attracted to this warmer water.*

The flats of the Susquehanna River at the head of the Chesapeake Bay are a great place to take striped bass on a fly in early May. At that time, stripers are prowling these shallow flats, hungry and eager to take flies. The Clouser Minnow and Lefty's Deceiver are favorite patterns of local anglers for these fish. Most of the fish will leave this area by early June.

I believe some of the best striped bass fishing on the East Coast is in Rhode Island. In mid May, the school stripers work the Bristol Narrows, Barrington's Hundred Acre Cove, and the western shore of the mouth of the Kickemuit River.

The larger stripers usually arrive along the Atlantic Coast from New Jersey to Massachusetts and Connecticut in late May or early June. They tend to lie just off the coast or in deeper bays, in drop-offs, or in underwater humps. When they move closer to land, they can be difficult to take on flies. They will strike small flies, but big baitfish imitations that are easy to cast will often produce more large fish. Bob Popovics' Siliclone Mullet, which imitates bigger menhaden, is one such pattern. The most productive fishing occurs late in the day or at dawn.

By mid June, striped bass are flooding into a number of rivers in Maine. The Kennebec River hosts an incredible number of fish from mid June until late July. A boat rigged with a depth finder is a decided asset here. This river is so deep that warships travel it to Bath, Maine, for refitting. By using a depth finder, you can locate the ledges and deep drop-offs and thus the schools of stripers holding in these areas. Of course, fish breaking the surface of the water can also be a tip-off. By far the best fly lines for fishing the Kennebec are those that sink quickly, such as the Teeny 300 and 400 lines.

By mid June, fly fishermen can catch stripers from Virginia to Maine. Cape Cod and Martha's Vineyard are two great spots to fly fish for stripers from mid June through October, and even into November if the weather is mild. During these summer and early fall months, the standard method for catching stripers is to watch out for fish breaking the surface of the water and place your cast in their immediate area. Calm seas and bright sunny days seem to cause the stripers to move away from the shorelines. The best fishing is along the beaches at dawn and dusk.

Stripers will even take flies all night long, and in New England a great number of fly rodders fish only at night during the summer. For me, however, night fishing holds little charm. I feel that fishing is a visual sport, and I enjoy seeing everything going on. I find night fishing is like fishing in the daytime with your eyes closed. I'm not knocking it. I simply don't enjoy it — and I fish for the enjoyment of the sport.

In the Chesapeake Bay, many of the largest fish become difficult targets from July through mid September, since the larger stripers tend to hold in deeper waters off channels. Smaller fish can be seen breaking throughout the summer. But the best fishing for larger stripers in the Chesapeake is from early May to mid June, and then from late September until late October or early November, depending on how warm the fall is. In Virginia, at the mouth of the Bay, the smaller two to 10-pound stripers can be found around the various structures of the Bay Bridge Tunnel system, along the edges of flats, and in the estuaries, throughout the summer and in early fall. In late October, larger fish begin clustering around the rock piles of the Bay Bridge Tunnel. By early December, the migrating fish have arrived and with them the chance to catch a trophy striped bass, so long as the weather is fairly warm. Anglers can keep trying even into early January.

In southern New England, September brings a change in fish movements and fishing tactics. Night fishing is still productive, but as water temperatures start to drop in mid to late September, there are hints of migrations of ducks, shorebirds — and some stripers. At this time, many school stripers swarm along the coast just south of Maine all the way through New Jersey. From Massachusetts to Long Island, four to five-inch mullet swarm in bays and along the rocky shorelines. Mullet are a favorite food of striped bass, and large Lefty's Deceivers or other easy-to-cast streamers that represent these baitfish will fool large striped bass. Mullet tend to swim just below the surface, creating telltale "nervous water." So popping bugs imitating this action can also be deadly on striped bass at this time.

October brings the southern New England coast's most productive striped bass fishing with a fly rod. From sometime in July on, the best action usually occurs at dusk or dawn. Maybe it's because they detect the coming of the fall and winter seasons, but for some reason the bass seem to feed more during the day at this time. Perhaps they are putting on a layer of fat for the cold months. At any rate, the bass are hungry, and they sometimes push the baitfish to the shorelines — even up onto the sand! Places such as Cape Cod and Martha's Vineyard can feature dynamite fishing from the beaches.

Also at this time of the year, many juvenile baitfish are swarming and beginning to move south. This means that in the fall the angler may be presented with many different sizes of baitfish. In these circumstances, while exact imitation is not necessary, approximately matching the length of your flies to that of the prevalent baitfish should result in better fishing success. If October is warm and November not too cold, great fishing from the beaches can be enjoyed in southern New England as late as Thanksgiving Day. Some intrepid fly fishermen have even caught stripers in early December.

Along the New Jersey coast, the migrating fish begin showing up in large numbers along the beaches in early November as they move out of the waters of New England and New York. If the weather doesn't turn too cold, good fishing can be enjoyed through late December.

GEAR AND TACKLE REQUIREMENTS

Striped bass fishing is done from the beach, from a boat, or from shallow flats, day and night. Because of the variety of conditions, anglers need some specialized gear.

Boats

Let's start with boats, since casting from them may be the way most striper fishermen go after their quarry. On the shallow flats of Florida, Louisiana, and Texas, specially designed boats are used to pole for permit, tarpon, redfish, and bonefish. These tropical flats boats are designed with low sides so that there isn't much "sail" area for the breeze. A boat with higher sides would also be much more difficult to pole.

In most cases, however, this type of boat is not the best for striped bass on the East Coast, from Virginia to Maine. Striper fishermen there often have to travel choppy waters, and in a low-sided tropical flats boat they can get very wet. I think an ideal boat for most striper fishing is between 18 and 20 feet long and relatively light, with fairly high sides for protection from the waves. The inside of the boat should have as few line-grabbing devices as possible. In other words, it is really a modification of the standard Florida flats boat.

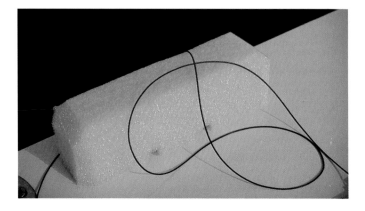

Cover a Cleat with a Foam Block

Captain Greg Weatherby charters out of Newport, Rhode Island. One feature I really liked on his boat was the bow rail, similar to the rail on a pulpit. The fly caster can stand inside this railing and lean against it. Then Greg can work his boat in close to the rocks where waves make the boat rise and fall. The railing offers full support, and with his hands free, the angler is able to cast in very rough water. The key to the success of this device, I believe, is to keep the railing design very narrow, just wide enough for the angler to slip in. Any wider, and the angler's body will sway and the railing may catch line during a cast.

If there are cleats on the boat, the best are those that fall flush with the surface of the boat when they are pushed in. If that's not the case, cut a small slot on the underside of a block of Ethafoam so that it can be jammed over the cleat. Taper the outer edges of the foam. If you make the slot small enough on the underside, the block will remain on the cleat even in a high-speed run. When Captain Norm Bartlett and I fished all day in the Chesapeake, our fly lines never once caught on the foam blocks on his boat.

Lines

In striper fishing, selecting the proper fly line can often mean the difference between catching fish and getting no strikes at all. I think you should seriously consider four kinds of lines: a weight-forward floater; a weight-forward intermediate (slow-sinking) line; a fast-sinking line, such as a lead-core shooting head or a line similar to the Teeny 300, 350, 400, or 450; and, if you're going to need to search a lot of water or cast long distances, a floating shooting line with a sinking shooting head. If I had to choose only one line for striped bass fishing (and thankfully I don't), I would choose one of the Teeny sinking lines.

Of course, floating lines are the easiest to fish with, but they are often a bother in the surf or where there is grass floating on the surface. Floating grass is often "funneled" down the floating line to the leader and onto the fly, ruining your retrieve. A floating line also undulates in the choppy water of the surf, and this can affect your retrieve. And a floating line fished with a streamer tends to loft the fly toward the surface every time line is drawn in on the retrieve.

Intermediate or fast-sinking lines are easier to cast in the wind because they are thinner in diameter. They will also get your fly deeper into the water column, and on the retrieve they tend to stay at the depth at which the retrieve began. This means that in the surf, the retrieve of the fly is less affected by wave action. And if there is floating grass, in most instances the line will slowly slide off the grass and drop below.

The Teeny series of lines (described in detail earlier in this book) are my favorites for fishing flies deeper. Only when I need to get the fly as deep as possible will I resort to a lead-core shooting head with a running line of 30-pound-test Amnesia monofilament.

Striped bass are generally not leader shy, so you don't need to use long or thin leaders. A tippet of 15 pounds will work most of the time. For floating and intermediate sinking lines, a leader of eight to 10 feet is fine. For fast-sinking fly lines, I rarely use a leader more than five feet long.

Reels

Since I first started fishing for them in the early 1960s, I have caught more than a thousand striped bass on a fly rod. While I have not caught a striper larger than 35 pounds, I have battled many stronger fish in the sea. So I am convinced that a reel that carries 150 yards of backing, plus the fly line, gives you more than enough line to fight just about any striped bass you will ever hook. In fact, in my opinion, few stripers — or almost any other saltwater fish, for that matter — will ever run more than 100 yards plus the length of your fly line.

Consequently, reels for striper fishing need not be the heavy-duties used on giant tarpon, bluefin tuna, or billfish. Obviously, if you can afford a Tibor, Lamson, Abel, Islander, Billy Pate, L.L. Bean Tidemaster, Orvis, or any other such reel, buy one. Not only will such a premier reel do more than it is ever called on to do, but it will give you a certain satisfaction to own, a fabulous tool. However, thousands of striped bass are caught on reels geared mainly for freshwater bass.

The reel needs just a little drag. If you can get a pound of drag on a straight pull, that's enough. By using your fingers on the rim of the reel or your fingertips on the inside of the spool to control drag, you can handle any striper up to 50 pounds on this outfit. Fly fishermen have always had a tendency to overgun themselves when they go to saltwater.

Rods

Rods are so good today that we old-timers wonder how we ever fished with the rods we used before. The best length rod is a 9-footer. This may be a little light for throwing very large striper flies, but it will do a commendable job in most striper fishing situations. Here again there is a tendency for some anglers to be overgunned and use 11 to 13-weight fly rods. If you are a great caster, that's fine. But the average guy is going to feel like dying after two hours of slinging a 12-weight line on a heavy rod. For almost all heavy-duty striped bass fishing, I rarely use anything larger than a 10-weight.

And again, keep in mind the modification I think should be made to all fly rods used in the salt: a stripping guide (the largest guide) of at least 20 mm — and that's the *smallest* diameter that anyone should consider for rods 7-weight and larger. For 9 through 12-weight rods, I favor a 25-mm.

Flies

There are a host of flies that will catch striped bass. Anglers tend to develop personal preferences for a few favorite patterns, and that's just fine. Also, it's fun and a valuable part of the fly fishing experience to tie new flies and hope to find that "secret" pattern that will catch more fish. However, you need only a few patterns to catch most striped bass in most situations, that is, if you are willing to vary length and color.

For most striped bass fishing, East or West Coast, if you have the following flies in different lengths and color combinations, you will be able to fish for stripers successfully, most of the time and under most conditions: Clouser Minnow, popping bug, Lefty's Deceiver, Whistler, and Bend Back.

As more and more trout fishermen enter the sport, they bring with them the idea of exact imitation. But there are rare situations, and these are very rare, when a very close imitation will outfish other patterns. Several dozen patterns, for example, have been developed that imitate sand eels in New England waters. But a properly dressed Clouser Minnow or Lefty's Deceiver would do just as well.

I've described the five patterns recommended above earlier in this book, but for more detail, you might check a few other sources. I've written a book that includes pictures of several dozen striped bass flies.* Along with each color photograph are instructions for tying the pattern. I am not mentioning this to sell books. But if you are interested in tying the striped bass patterns you hear about, most can be found in these pages.

Also, a companion volume in this Library, *The Professionals' Favorite Flies, Volume II,* includes descriptions and recipes for a number of patterns that are very effective on stripers and other saltwater fish.

One point that anglers should remember when fishing flies to striped bass is that large stripers will often hit a large fly more readily than a smaller fly. As a result, there are some flies out there that look like overdressed chickens and would take someone with the arm of a wrestler to throw any distance. But these huge patterns are unnecessary, and I urge you to avoid using them.

If you feel you need more flies than I have discussed here, you might try some of Bob Popovics' patterns. Bob has developed several different flies that present a huge profile (representing squid or baitfish such as bunker or menhaden), are light and easy to cast, and appear realistic in the water. His Siliclone Mullet and Baby Squid are two of the best patterns I have ever used to fool big striped bass.

Stripping Baskets

Perhaps the best tool a striped bass fishermen can own, once he has assembled the proper rod, reel, line, and fly, is a stripping basket. The fly line can be a major problem for an angler fishing from the beach or shoreline. If the line drops into the surf, it becomes a hopeless tangle. On a jetty or rock

---

Salt Water Fly Patterns (Lyons & Burford, Publishers, 31 West 21 Street, New York, NY 10010, 1995).

pile, the stones frequently grab the line and halt it in midflight. A stripping basket solves these problems.

Stripping baskets used in a boat can alleviate casting difficulties, too. When there is a stiff breeze, a stripping basket virtually eliminates line-tangling problems for the fisherman in the bow. However, unless there is a strong breeze blowing the line around, I prefer to drop the line to the deck rather than use a stripping basket when casting from the bow of a boat designed for fly fishing. But for the angler who must fish from the rear of a boat, a stripping basket is a godsend! This is because there are generally a host of little things at the stern of most boats that grab the fly line and spoil the cast.

A stripping basket is usually a plastic container worn on a belt or other attachment on the angler. Line is dropped into the basket during the retrieve. Properly designed baskets will normally have heavy monofilament stubs sticking up from the bottom, or better, monofilament in the shape of miniature horseshoes. These stubs or horseshoes hold the line in place. When the cast is made, the line almost always flows

Drop Line on the Lower Deck of a Boat — Never on the Casting Platform

A Bucket Can Be Used as a Stripping Basket

smoothly from the basket. Orvis makes a good stripping basket that replaces the stubs or horseshoes with inverted cones that work just fine.

If you want to construct your own stripping basket, you should be familiar with the two basic stripping-basket designs that have been developed.

The most popular stripping basket, which is designed to be attached to the front of your waist, is made from a rectangular plastic container approximately 14 inches long, 10 inches wide, and 6 inches deep — a dishpan, if you will. Inserted in the bottom of the interior of the basket are a dozen or so single plastic stubs (or stubs doubled over, folded into the "U" shape of a horseshoe), preferably made from the type of heavy-duty nylon used in weed-cutting garden tools, though 100-pound monofilament works fine. To install the single stubs or doubled horseshoe-shaped pieces of heavy monofilament in the bottom of the container, pierce one hole per stub (or two holes for each horseshoe shape) using a drill or a heated nail of an appropriate size. Insert the stubs or horseshoes and hold them in place with hot glue, applying Goop or other glue to seal them in position permanently.

This basket is secured against the angler's stomach by a belt or elastic cord around the waist. The angler makes the cast, tucks the rod under his arm, and begins a hand-over-hand retrieve. The basket is small and fairly portable, but having the rod under your arm during the retrieve is not so handy when you want to strike. And the hand-over-hand retrieve required does restrict movement to a small degree.

The stripping basket design I much prefer is slightly larger and deeper and hangs on your side. This hip basket is a standard plastic wastebasket approximately 18 inches high, with the opening at the top about 8 inches by 15 inches. Plastic stubs are installed in the bottom, and several fairly large holes are also cut in the bottom to allow water drainage. The basket is secured by a shoulder harness and a leg strap. The leg strap has a Velcro closure and fits above the knee. If you need to run down the beach, this basket won't be a hindrance.

Norm Bartlett, the captain who plies his trade on the Chesapeake Bay, showed me his improvement on this stripping basket. His basket has a large number of rectangular holes or ports in all four sides, which reduce the basket's weight and allow water to drain more quickly.

The hip basket offers several advantages over a stripping basket worn at the waist. In the hip design, the line never falls out after it has been dropped inside, unlike the waist design. The hip basket also allows me to retrieve line normally. I find that while I can strip-strike with a rod tucked under my arm, I am more efficient when I'm using a basket that is attached on the side. The one situation I think the belly basket is better than the hip basket is when the surf is heavy. If you haven't used a hip-type stripping basket, I urge you to try it.

Overleaf: *Nick Zoll with a nice barracuda.*

CHAPTER SIX

FISHING FOR OTHER INSHORE SPECIES

ALBACORE

Along the United States' East Coast, from South Carolina to New England, there is a fish tailor-made for fly fishing, a species of tuna, the albacore. When hooked, this fish is like chained lightning.

Albacore travel in schools of eight to more than 50, chasing small bait such as bay anchovies at high speed. Albacore arrive in New England waters in early summer and unfortunately are not often found close to the beaches during June, July, and August. When they are found off the beaches in the summer, it may well take a fast boat to catch up to them, and then only a few casts can be made before the fish move on. It can be frustrating.

However, in late September things change. The albacore start pushing bait right up on the beaches of New England and down the coast to New Jersey. Some of the Northeast's most exciting saltwater fly fishing occurs in September and October as these fish migrate south to warmer waters.

Never have I seen albacore concentrate as they do off Cape Lookout in North Carolina, which is about 40 miles south of the famed Outer Banks and not far from Morehead City. Tom Earnhardt introduced me to this fishing. Running from

Harker's Island in his boat, we approached the open sea near the Cape Lookout lighthouse. The mouth of the inlet was covered with thousands of albacore. While in waters farther north a good-sized albacore weighs 12 pounds, here that's the size of an average fish, and Tom knows of albacore, weighed on a commercial scale, that topped 20 pounds! The concentrations begin in mid October and last until it gets pretty chilly in late November.

Flies for albacore are very simple. They must imitate the smaller baitfish that albacore seek. One of the best flies is a small Clouser Minnow no longer than the average man's ring finger. The wing should be dressed with Ultra Hair, and at least eight to 10 strands of pearl Flashabou or Crystal Flash should be added. Dress the bottom of the wing with clear or smoke-colored Ultra Hair. Add the flash material, then make the top wing of either pale blue or green, dark blue, green, or chartreuse. The chartreuse-and-white combination seems to work especially well when the waters are a little dirty. The other patterns work best under clear water conditions.

The eyes on the Clouser Minnow are very important! Use metallic eyes and paint them silver or aluminum with a large, dark pupil. Most of the baitfish that the albacore are pursuing have a pronounced eye; flies dressed with eyes unlike those I've just described don't seem to produce as well.

Since albacore, like other tuna, have exceptional eyesight, you need to fish with a leader no larger than 15-pound test; a 10 to 12-pound-test is recommended. Under very clear conditions, fluorocarbon tippets will draw more strikes.

Tackle has to be fairly stout — a 9-weight rod is my choice. But what is even more important with these powerful fish is a good reel with a smooth drag. Unlike the reel used on most other inshore species, a reel for albacore should be loaded with at least 200 yards of backing. This is one fish that will definitely get into your backing — and fast!

One caution when catching these wonderful fly-rod fish: don't keep them out of the water for even a minute or two. If you are going to photograph an albacore, have everything ready, lift the fish, click the camera, and get the fish back in the water immediately. *If at all possible, do not lift an albacore from the water when removing the hook.* In order to keep oxygenated water flowing at a high rate over their gills, tuna must never stop swimming during their lifetime. Keep these fish out of the water even a few minutes and they will likely die.

If you must lift an albacore from the water, don't replace it as you would other fish. Instead, hold the albacore at an angle with the fish's head pointed downward. Then throw the fish headfirst into the water so that it strikes the water in a steep dive. This better insures that the fish will recover and swim away.

REDFISH

The redfish, or channel bass, is one of the most popular game-fishes among coastal fishermen. From Texas to South Carolina, fly fishermen refer to it as redfish. In North Carolina, small channel bass are called puppy drum and large ones just red drum. Most fly fishermen use the term redfish, especially when talking about channel bass less than 20 pounds. Redfish are caught from New Jersey down the eastern coast and around Florida, and all the way up the Gulf of Mexico into Texas. In Florida and the Gulf States redfish average from two to 10 pounds, with an occasional specimen going to 15 pounds or larger.

From mid to late May and into June, schools of huge channel bass usually work the shallows inside North Carolina's Oregon Inlet and the flats on either side of Davis Strait. Boats on these shallow banks can locate these husky fish, some of which top 60 pounds. For these monsters, you will need to use a very large Lefty's Deceiver-type fly, eight inches or longer, dressed on a #5/0 hook, and at least a 12-weight line.

It is not generally known, but during the summer months until the first hard frost, smaller channel bass roam the inside or western flats in many places south of Oregon Inlet.

There is terrific redfishing in the shallow estuaries around Charleston, South Carolina; these estuaries are filled with oyster bars and a lot of baitfish and shrimp. In the lower end of Pamlico Sound, North Carolina, you find redfish in water so shallow they create a wake as they swim. Hilton Head, South Carolina, has such a good population of redfish on the flats that several top guides are kept busy. Around Titusville is some of the best redfishing in Florida. Poling a canoe or small boat across the flats can lead to wonderful sight fishing.

Most rewarding for fly fishermen has been the comeback of redfish and snook in Florida, as well as the return of redfish to their native flats in Louisiana and Texas. This was all due to pressure placed by the fishermen of that region on their politicians to create laws for controlling the harvest of redfish. As in the case of the striped bass along the Atlantic Coast, as soon as better fishery management was introduced, the fish came back in astonishing numbers. Redfishing in Texas, Louisiana, and Florida is better now than it has been for decades.

Florida Bay redfishing is great from late April through October, but many redfish remain on the flats all year. They leave when a cold spell hits and the water drops into the 50s. But they return again as soon as waters warm.

Farther up the coast and along the shore of Louisiana are many shallow oyster bars and flats that hold large numbers of channel bass. When waters are clear and the winds abate, especially in Texas, the fly rodder can have excellent fishing.

The Texas coast has miles of shallow flats that are somewhat like those of upper Florida Bay. The redfish, along with seatrout, furnish the major flats' targets for Texas fly fishermen. Here anglers skim over the water in shallow-draft boats and fish much the same way fishermen do in Florida. Many of the flats are grass-covered, and the fish, which are a little larger than those in Florida, can be seen swimming and tailing. One good spot is the flats in the Laguna Madre area of south Texas. The fish are there all summer, but April and May are the choice months.

Channel bass don't have the superior eyesight that permit and bonefish have, so the fly rodder must cast his fly close enough for the fish to see it — but not close enough to alarm. Throw the fly six to 10 feet ahead of the fish, then retrieve it so that the paths of the fly and the cruising fish intersect. You should cast to tailing redfish the same way you cast to bonefish. Drop the fly in front of and within 18 inches of the fish. As the redfish tips back to a normal swimming position, move the fly slowly in front of it.

Redfish will take almost any color fly, but the combinations of orange and red, olive and brown, chartreuse and white, olive and yellow, and red and white have all been productive. These patterns are also easy for the angler to see, so it's not difficult to keep track of the fly as it approaches the fish. The Clouser Minnow has become the most popular of all patterns for redfish. Since redfish are frequently found on grass-choked flats, a weedguard is often added to the pattern.

In Florida Bay, you can see redfish swimming right in the grass. At low tide, they will often be swimming in just six inches of water. Even with a weedguard, conventional flies work poorly because they are constantly entangling in the grassy bottom. To counteract that situation, two underwater patterns (both of which are on my essential saltwater-pattern list) have been developed that work exceptionally well.

One is the Bend Back. The wing consists of a liberal amount of bucktail or fluffy marabou of the colors recommended above. An ample amount of strips of Flashabou or Crystal Flash aids the redfish in locating the fly. This is a simple fly, but you can drag it through the grass with only a very few hang-ups, especially when the hook shank is left bare.

The other fly is the Seaducer, a hackle streamer. It works something like a dry fly, in that the palmer-wound hackles along the hook shank support the fly so well it cannot sink far below the surface. In fact, if several false casts are made, the angler frequently has to jerk the fly to get it to drop below the surface. Once underwater, the fly sits almost suspended, the hackles on the shank flexing back and forth and the saddle feathers at the rear working in a way that excites any channel bass that sees it. Because of its buoyancy, the pattern can be manipulated in inches of water, and the palmer-wound hackles usually brush the fly away from most grass, making it relatively weedproof.

A popping bug works wonders sometimes, but at other times it just scares the hell out of the fish. So early in every fishing day, it's a good idea to test the redfish's reaction to your popper patterns. When a popper pattern is working, color seems unimportant. The trick is to cast the popper four to six feet away from the fish, and then make soft popping sounds with it (instead of loud splashing noises) to attract the fish.

The problem with using poppers and Dahlberg Diver-type fly patterns on redfish is that because the mouth of a redfish is located low on its head to allow the fish to feed well on the bottom, the redfish often has difficulty grabbing the fly, and missed strikes frequently occur.

The redfish is not known for its fighting ability. Once hooked, it will make short determined runs and then stand on its head and try to rub the fly out against the bottom. Saltwater fly fishermen often use shock leaders of 15 to 30-pound test because of this grubbing maneuver, but most of the time the redfish can be taken on a conventional leader.

A considerable number of light-tackle spinning specialists in Texas have been fishing these channel bass for years. But now more and more fly rodders are beginning to experience the joys of seeking this fine sportfish.

BLUEFISH

For years the bluefish has been one of the prime targets for inshore fly fishermen from the mid-Atlantic region to New England. Bluefish are found worldwide; in Africa, New Zealand, and Australia, they are called tailors. On the East Coast of the United States, the fish range from Florida to Maine, the greatest numbers being found in the stretch from North Carolina to Connecticut.

It is not generally realized that bluefish populations are cyclic. Every 40 years the numbers peak, then decline sharply, then slowly rise as the cycle continues. I am not certain what causes these peaks and valleys, but I would guess they are connected to the supply of baitfish, as no northern fish feeds more voraciously than bluefish.

The bluefish populations along the Atlantic Coast peaked in the late 1980s. At that time there were incredible numbers of bluefish, and many caught on a fly exceeded 16 pounds. Since the early 1990s, however, the population has really declined, but that's not to say there aren't quite a few of them around. While large bluefish are now very scarce, small blues from one pound to about six pounds are often encountered by fly fisherman.

Of the many ways to fish for bluefish with a fly, none approaches the effectiveness of chumming. Bluefish are roamers, constantly on the move, so trying to run them down is difficult. Even when they are breaking and feeding on the surface, they are only up for a short period of time before diving back below the surface. But if you set yourself up to chum for bluefish, their insatiable appetite will generally lure them right to you.

Many foods can be used for chum. A frozen block of ground fish can be hung overboard; as the block slowly melts, bits of the fish are released to drift with the tidal current. Some people dribble fish oil overboard, but I've had little luck with this. Another trick is to boil elbow macaroni and mix it with dry oatmeal, then slowly stream this chum overboard. But while this attracts some bluefish, my experience is that it is only a so-so way of getting blues into your chum line.

The very best chum is ground baitfish (not frozen), such as menhaden or alewives. Many local fish houses or marinas will sell it to you. Even better is baitfish that is fresh-caught — the fresher the better.

To prepare chum from whole baitfish, the standard method is to feed the fish whole into a sausage grinder attached to the side of the boat. The ground mass of meat is then placed overboard, one large spoonful at a time, enough to keep the bluefish in the chum line. Don't chum too heavily; the fish may feed too well and ignore your artificial fly, or just leave after they are full.

Tackle requirements for bluefish are simple but specific. It's best to have two fly-line outfits: one with a sink-tip, the other one a sinking head or full-sinking line. (Floating fly lines are very ineffective.) Hooks should be in the #1 to #2/0 range. You will need to tie on a bite leader to prevent cut-offs, since bluefish have very sharp teeth. Heavy monofilament (40 to 80-pound test) can work well on smaller bluefish, but I have lost a number of bluefish weighing more than 14 pounds with this material. I now use either braided wire (30-pound-test) or solid stainless steel trolling wire. The braided wire that is easiest to use is coated with nylon. However, bluefish will frequently strip some of the coating from the wire, leaving strands of dangling nylon that spook the fish and reduce the number of strikes. If you are fishing in relatively clear water, use a wire bite leader no longer than four inches. Longer than that will deter the fish from hitting.

Rod size is your choice. Unless the blues are unusually heavy, a 7 or 8-weight rod is fine for use in a chum line. If you are fishing from a jetty or to running or breaking fish, you may want to use a 9-weight rod.

Fly fishing in a chum line is considerably like nymphing for trout. *The key is to have the right fly and to float it at the same depth and speed as the chum that is being ladled overboard.* The right fly is the Bloody Chum Fly, a very easy pattern to tie. Wrap about four turns of heavy fuse wire (.030) on the shank of a #1 or #2/0 hook. At the front, tie in some medium-brown marabou to form a skirt around the hook. The marabou need not be longer than 1 1/2 inches. On another fly, wrap the entire hook shank with .030 wire. This gives you two flies of different sink rates. Attach a four-inch length of wire between the four or five-foot monofilament leader and the chum fly.

If the current is not running too fast, use a sink-tip line. If the tidal flow is fairly fast, use either a sinking head or a full-sinking line. Drop your fly where the chum is thrown on the surface, and swing the rod tip so that the fly swims at the same speed and depth as the chum. You may have to put on a heavier or faster sinking line and fly to achieve the proper drift. As the tidal flow increases or decreases, simply adjust your line and fly weight to get the proper drift. Your goal is to have the chum and fly float together. *Never strip or retrieve the fly —* let it float naturally.

Just as you would in nymphing for trout, watch the line, and if it stops or darts in any direction, set the hook.

This is a simple technique to learn, and it is an extremely effective one. In fact, with it I have frequently out-fished spin fishermen who were using live baitfish.

SNOOK

Back in the 1970s, when I was associate editor of *Florida Sportsman Magazine,* we conducted a poll among our readers, asking them for the name of their favorite fish. The snook won hands down.

I believe one reason for the snook's popularity is that it has a lot in common with our very popular largemouth bass. And millions of anglers who live in Florida spent much of the earlier part of their lives in largemouth country. The difference between the two fish is that the snook is a much tougher adversary. It has exceptionally keen eyesight, lives in fresh, brackish, and saltwater, and fights much harder than any largemouth bass I have ever caught.

I think that a snook in clear water is one of the most difficult fish to fool with a lure or fly.

During the 1980s the snook declined drastically due to overfishing. However, regulations were enacted and the snook has now recovered. In fact, both snook fishing and redfishing are better now than they were in the early 1960s when I first moved to south Florida.

It's interesting that much of the snook's decline in numbers was attributed to the taste of its flesh. Many years ago, people simply did not eat snook, calling it the "soap fish" because it tasted like soap. Then someone discovered that if you skin the fish, the soapy taste is eliminated. Today, most people who have eaten snook maintain that it tastes better than any other fish out there.

Snook are more affected by the phases of the moon than most inshore fish. You may locate snook hanging around a certain spot during a neap tide and then come back a few days later to find they have disappeared. What this means is that if you fish an area frequently, you should keep a record of where the fish are located during various tidal phases.

Snook are also sensitive to cold. I have never found snook feeding or swimming in the shallows when the water temperature was below 68 degrees. Warm waters don't seem to bother the fish as much; good snook fishing often occurs in waters in the 80-degree range.

Snook prefer to feed at night. However, most snook are caught during daylight hours, so don't think that daytime fishing has to be unproductive.

These fish tend to hang out near cover — mangrove roots, pilings, wharfs and piers, drop-offs at oyster bars and gravel bars, and around markers, buoys, and just about any structure where they can hide and ambush their prey.

Some of my favorite places to fly fish for snook are white holes or potholes. On most grass-covered flats there exist these depressions, usually pale white or cream, with no grass growing in them. Both snook and larger seatrout will hold in these potholes and ambush any fly that is cast to them.

In Florida, particularly along the lower west coast, the snook migrate in the spring to the passes or channels that drain the many bays along the shore. They seem to go on a feeding binge in preparation for early summer spawning. Snook also migrate along the beaches; you can frequently see them swimming within a few feet of the dry sand, especially on high spring tides, early or late in the day. This sight fishing can be really exciting and rewarding. Some of the largest snook are caught in May.

Being poled along a mangrove-lined shoreline and casting your fly among the tangled roots is a very pleasant saltwater fly-fishing activity. But casting is a dangerous sport here. The spider-like legs of the red mangrove trees act as a mesh net. Any miscalculation means a good chance of snagging your fly. This type of fishing requires accurate casting of the highest order.

Best of all (or worst, for some anglers) is that snook usually must be caught from a distance. They seem to be very sensitive to the shock waves sent out by the rocking of a boat as the angler works his false cast. Even the slight noise a guide has to make in quietly pushing the boat along will spook the wary fish. So it is always best to cast to snook from as great a distance as you can handle.

Having said all that, the snook is a worthy target and can be caught frequently on flies. In many situations, the fly is actually superior to other artificial lures. Fly selection is not difficult; presentation is much more critical. Fortunately, snook seem to enjoy hitting a floating fly, so a popping bug or Dahlberg Diver is always a good choice, except in very shallow and clear water, when a surface disturbance may actually frighten them. I recommend using the Seaducer in very shallow and clear water. This pattern can be dropped close to a wary snook and fished more slowly than any underwater fly I know of.

When casting to docks, piers, or mangrove roots, you must get the fly close to the cover or even into it. Naturally, this will increase your chances of snagging the hook. For this reason, many snook fishermen prefer to use one of two flies. One is the Glades Deceiver, a modified Lefty's Deceiver typically dressed on a #2, #1, or #1/0 hook. The feather wing is rarely longer than three inches, usually shorter. There are several strands of Mylar flash material on each side. The collar is usually made from calftail, although fine-diameter bucktail works, too. The important component is a wire weedguard. Generally preferred is #5 (.014 in diameter) stainless steel trolling wire. A few tyers use #4 wire, which is slightly thinner.

The other pattern that works so well for casting to hook-snagging structure is the Bend Back fly. This fly rides with the hook up, and the wing encases the hook.

If either the Glades Deceiver or the Bend Back gets into a likely snagging area, fish it very slowly. The wire weedguard or the inverted hook will simply crawl through and come free.

If you jerk on the fly that you've thrown into branches or among snags, the hook will probably hang up.

For the Glades Deceiver, Bend Back, and Seaducer, there are a few color combinations that seem to provoke the most strikes from snook. The combination of red and white does well, as does olive and brown. Sometimes yellow and red works, too. I always add a little flash material to the sides of these flies. As for popping bugs and Dahlberg Divers, I believe color is unimportant. It's not the color but how you work a surface lure that turns on a snook.

BARRACUDA

Few strikes are more exciting in saltwater fly fishing than those of a barracuda. A 'cuda will put an Atlantic salmon to shame when it comes to speed and jumping ability. I have seen 'cudas streak out of the water at a low angle and travel 20 feet through the air, then a few seconds later repeat the leap!

The best barracuda fishing occurs during the winter months in Florida, the Bahamas, and other parts of that subtropical zone. Of course, there are always some 'cudas around, but when the water cools a bit, the bigger ones tend to drift in from the open water and cruise the shallows. This is the time to connect with a true trophy.

For many years we threw skinny needlefish flies to barracuda. The damned things would always tangle. One fish was usually all you could catch before your fly was ruined. Worse, the needlefish pattern presented such a sleek profile that I'm not sure many 'cudas even saw it. On top of this, we retrieved the fly as fast as we could, since the barracuda is so swift. If you have ever seen how slowly an angler makes a hand-over-hand retrieve of his fly, compared to how quickly a 'cuda can streak in toward it, you know our efforts were futile.

Two Great Barracuda Flies

I began experimenting a few years ago and have now decided on a technique that I feel is vastly superior to the hand-over-hand retrieving technique used for so long. This new method requires a different kind of fly, a weight-forward floating fly line, and an entirely different retrieve.

The fly I now use is much different than the needlefish fly. I tie one pattern in two different color combinations, and I use both forms for sharks, as well. To tie the fly, place a #1/0 hook in the vise. You don't need a large hook; the 'cuda will inhale the entire fly in its big maw. Turn the hook upside down in the vise (point up, shank down) and tie in a liberal amount of the longest bucktail you have. The bottom of the wing can be all white or all yellow. Turn the fly over to the normal position in the vise and add 20 or 30 strands of gold or copper Flashabou on top of the underwing. If you have tied white bucktail as the underwing, tie in chartreuse as the upper wing. If you used yellow bucktail as the underwing, then add a wing of bright red bucktail after tying in the Flashabou.

That's all you have to do. I call one fly Lefty's Shark/Cuda Fly White/Chartreuse and the other Lefty's Shark/Cuda Fly Yellow/Red.

Once you have this fly, which presents a rather big profile, you're ready to seek out a 'cuda. When you find one, using a weight-forward floating line cast the fly about four feet in front of the fish. As soon as the fly touches the surface, draw it several feet through the water and then make an *immediate* back cast. Repeat this by dropping the fly back four feet in front of the 'cuda and making another immediate back cast. Don't let the fly settle on the water; as soon as it touches down, make another back cast. On the third cast, allow the fly to drop to the water and then begin an erratic retrieve. It doesn't have to be fast, but the fly must be kept in constant action.

Barracudas are hard to fool, with their keen sight and their ability to swiftly overtake a fish. But this method works more often than any other I have tried.

There is one other retrieve that often works, too. Drop a popping bug on the surface well in front of the 'cuda, that is, 10 to 15 feet. *Never* throw the popper close to the 'cuda — the bug will almost always frighten it. Try to keep the popper moving constantly. As with my two 'cuda flies, it is not the speed of retrieve that counts but the constant gurgling, popping, and moving of the bug.

Obviously, for all 'cuda presentations you need to tie a piece of wire bite leader just in front of the fly or popping bug. Few teeth are sharper than a 'cuda's. But the type of wire and how long you make it are important in drawing strikes. I rarely use solid wire larger than #4, which is about 40-pound-test and more than adequate. Braided wire is larger in diameter so I try to avoid using it, but if I do, I don't use larger than 30-pound test. The length of the bite leader wire is critical. Five inches of wire is the maximum, and four inches is even better. Rarely have I been cut off with a four-inch wire bite leader.

Not highly regarded by many people who fish the flats of Florida and other tropical waters is the shark. Yet in my opinion, it can be one of the most difficult fish to catch on a fly. If you have ever poled across a flat after what appears to be a slow-swimming shark, you have learned that it's not slow-moving at all. Despite appearances, that shark is moving along pretty fast.

There are two ways to fish for sharks on the flats. In both, a silent approach is required since a shark's sense of hearing is acute. One way is to see a shark swimming and make a cast. This is opportunistic fishing and is perhaps the least effective way to catch sharks.

The other and best way works almost anytime that sharks are in your vicinity. Catch a fish — preferably a barracuda, but any fish will do — and attach it to about 20 feet of line. With the bait dragging behind, pole or drift the boat in an area that is frequented by sharks. Watch carefully behind the boat. If there are any sharks in the area, they will almost always be lured in.

When the shark is within a few feet of the dead fish, have someone bring it quickly into the boat. Now make a cast. Since a shark has poor eyesight and its mouth is located well back from the front of its head, you need to make the cast alongside the shark's eye. For if the fly is thrown to a normal position in front of the shark, the front of the shark's head gets in the way when it tries to grab the fly. Casting near the eye is especially important if you are using popping bugs. Poppers certainly will encourage a shark to strike, but the front of a shark's head will generally push a popping bug away from the strike zone.

My favorite fly patterns for sharks are the two just mentioned for barracuda, the Lefty's Shark/Cuda flies. They need

Cast to a Shark Near Its Eye

to be made large enough for the shark, with its poor eyesight, to see easily. I prefer the hooks to be #2/0 for sharks weighing more than 20 pounds. I believe that a #3/0 hook is often too difficult to drive into the tough mouth of a shark.

Solid wire is the *only* wire to use for bite leaders. Braided wire can cost you a good fish. During a long fight, the teeth of the shark will cut one of the thin strands of a braided-wire leader, and then another, and so on. Eventually, enough strands will be cut to weaken the wire sufficiently for the shark to break free.

Some people chum sharks with great success, but I have had only poor results. I do know that in deeper water, such as off the coast of California, chumming works well.

APPENDIX

In the Introduction to this book, I suggested there was really not much I could tell you about the techniques of fly fishing for teased billfish that you wouldn't learn in your first hour on the boat from an experienced captain and mate.

But I wouldn't want any member of this Library to report to his friends that Lefty had nothing whatsoever to say about the subject! I've done a good bit of fly fishing for sailfish and marlin, and if I have learned anything, I have learned that more than any other type of fly fishing, tackle is the most important ingredient recipe for success on these giant billfish. So I'd like to share a few tackle tips with you.

RODS

If you are familiar with hardware fishing for big game fish in saltwater, you know that short rods, those usually no longer than six or seven feet, are the norm on most offshore boats. This is because a short rod, contrary to what is generally believed, can punish a big fish much more effectively than a long one.

But for most fly fishermen it is difficult to cast a large billfish fly with a short rod. Also, the fly-fishing billfish market is so small that manufacturers have been quite reluctant to develop a line of heavyweight fly rods in short lengths for this rather specialized fly fishing. However, the top manufacturers are now producing a few excellent fly rods in longer lengths for billfish.

If you plan to obtain a billfish rod from a commercial source, you should plan on purchasing a graphite rod that is 8 1/2 to 9 feet in length and is no lighter than 11-weight, preferably 12 or 13-weight. Most graphite rods manufactured in these weights feature an extra-heavy butt section for fighting big fish and a relatively stiff action that aids in casting large and wind-resistant billfish fly patterns.

REELS

For this fishing, you must equip yourself with a large-capacity big-game saltwater fly reel. Whether the reel you select is direct-drive or anti-reverse, it must have a smooth and responsive drag system and be capable of storing the fly line plus at least 300 yards of backing. The bad news about these reels is that they are expensive. The large size IV models range in price from $400 to $600 (and even higher). The good news is that there are a number of superb models on the market for you to choose from. A few of the best-known brand names: Abel Big Game Reels, Stu Apte's ATH Saltwater Fly Reels, Fin-Nor, Islander, Billy Pate Reels, and SeaMaster.

LINES

The best billfish lines are specially designed for this fishing. They have a very heavy forward section followed by a rather thin but strong running line. Billfish swim so fast when trying to escape that a thicker running line creates enough drag to break many tippets. Several companies make a billfish line and indicate that it is for this type of fishing.

If you don't want to buy a commercial line, you can make your own. Cut off the first 40 feet of a fast-sinking line. Connect the remaining line to 100 feet of 30-pound monofilament. Then connect the rear end of the monofilament to the backing on the reel. This 100-foot section acts like a giant rubber band. Billfish have a tendency to leap a great deal. Too often the fish has leaped, jolted against the leader, and fallen back into the water before the angler has a chance to react. The jolts can easily snap the leader. With the 100-foot section of monofilament between the rear of the fly line and the backing, the angler has some insurance against a break-off.

The color of the monofilament is important. Monofilament that is hard to see won't work. Your boat captain will have to follow the billfish, and if he can't see the mono, he may run over it and cut it with the boat. I prefer fishing with bright orange or yellow monofilament backing. Both of these colors contrast nicely with the dark blue water.

BACKING

For many years, 30-pound Dacron has been used effectively as backing for billfish work. However, some of the new gel-spun polyethylene lines are now coming into favor. Use 50-pound-test — no less. These lines are very thin for their strength, and their smaller diameter will cause the line to dig into the bed of line on the spool and jam, resulting in a lost fish. A good combination is a base of Dacron backing and no more than 200 yards of gel-spun polyethylene line, such as Spider Wire. Also, gel-spun line has considerably less stretch than Dacron. When a hooked fish makes a wide, sweeping turn, the gel-spun line will follow the fish in a more direct path than the Dacron line would, thus creating less damaging drag. But remember to use firm pressure when placing any gel-spun polyethylene line on your reel spool, to prevent it from digging into the line beneath.

LEADERS AND TIPPETS

A standard tarpon rig — that is, a length of terminal 80 or 100-pound shock tippet (to which the fly pattern will be attached) followed by a class tippet, followed by the butt section (to which the fly line or shooting head is attached) — is the most widely used rigging for billfish. For more details on constructing this particular type of big-game saltwater leader, refer to two other companion books in the Library: *Fly Fishing for Bonefish, Permit & Tarpon* (pp. 129-131) and *Fly Fishing Knots and Connections* (pp. 110-116).

FLIES

Fly fishing for billfish requires that the fish first be lured near the boat by a teaser. The teaser infuriates the fish and draws it close enough so that a fly can be presented. Two types of flies are commonly used for this — popping bugs and streamers. Poppers draw immediate attention, but sometimes the bill of the fish knocks the fly away, causing a missed strike. Streamers seem to get better hook-ups, but the fish doesn't focus on a streamer as quickly as it does on a noisy popping bug. Some anglers therefore combine the two designs, tying on a large streamer pattern and then adding a detachable popper to the front of the fly.

I believe that the best billfish patterns will carry two hooks, one positioned up and the other down. Standard hooks for billfish run from #4/0 to #7/0, and there are good arguments for individual selections. Almost all experienced billfishermen open the gape on the hook slightly by bending it, so that the hook can get a better purchase in the billfish's mouth.

Most billfish flies are white-red, orange, or blue and white, although other color combinations can be effective. Here are a few of the most popular patterns:

Len Bearden's Sailfish Fly, basically a large (8-inch wing) Lefty's Deceiver with some modifications.

Billy Pate's Marlin Fly, a simple and rather crude-looking fly on a smaller hook than is normally used. But Billy has caught a number of billfish on this fly, including two world records on black marlin, so who can argue with that success?

Terry Baird's Deep Water Squid, light for its size. Terry says the basic idea for this pattern came from a pattern developed by Dan Blanton, called the Sea Arrow Squid.

Ralph Kanz's Mylar Minnow, a great offshore fly that has been tested for years.

Ralph Kanz's Bucktail Baitfish, another great pattern from one of our best saltwater fly tyers.

Lefty's Big-Eyed Deceiver, the familiar fly pattern tied on a #5/0 to #7/0 hook, with two large Ethafoam popper heads.

Winston Moore's Sailfish Flies, a series of patterns tied by the man who has caught more billfish on the fly than anyone else — at last count it was more than 100!

Worldwide Sportsman's Squid Fly.

Grant King's Sailfish Fly.

Rod Harrison's Billfish Fly, a very effective pattern developed by Rod Harrison, Australia's foremost saltwater fly fisherman. It is quite typical of conventional billfish fly patterns with its distinctive long streamer body, tandem hooks, and detachable popper. Instructions for tying this particular pattern may be found in a companion volume in the Library, *The Professionals' Favorite Flies, Volume II,* pp. 167-169.

Many of these flies and other favorite billfish patterns may be purchased or custom-tied by fly shops specializing in salt-

Four Billfish Flies — from top: *Squid Fly, Winston Moore's Sailfish Fly, Lefty's Deceiver, Lefty's Deceiver with Ethafoam.*

water fishing, such as Bob Marriott's Flyfishing Store in Fullerton, California (805-535-6633); International Angler in Pittsburgh, Pennsylvania (Tom Ference, 800-782-2222); Worldwide Sportsman, in Islamorada, Florida (800-327-2880); or The Saltwater Angler in Key West, Florida (Jeffrey Cardenas, 800-223-1629).

When you order your billfish flies, be prepared to spend some money. As I've said, everything about fly fishing for billfish is big, including the cost. Also, take a large arsenal of flies with you. One fly per hook-up is not unusual, as these big fish can really demolish your terminal tackle.

INDEX

FLY FISHING THE INSHORE WATERS

Designed by Robin McDonald, Birmingham, Alabama.

Cover photograph of a sunset at Dogfish Bay
off the coast of Martha's Vineyard by Sam Talarico.

Color photography by:
R. Valentine Atkinson/Frontiers (pages 2 and 100)
Lefty Kreh (page 19)
Flip Pallot (page 9)
Sam Talarico (pages 12, 26, 36, 49, 60, 71, 84).

Illustrated by Rod Walinchus, Livingston, Montana.

Text composed in Berkeley Old Style by Compos-it,
Montgomery, Alabama.

Film prepared by Compos-it, Montgomery, Alabama.

Color separations by Photographics,
Birmingham, Alabama.

Printed and bound by Quebecor Printing.

Text sheets are acid-free Warren Gloss by
S.D. Warren Company, a division of Scott Paper
Company, Boston, Massachusetts.

Endleaves are Rainbow Antique.

Cover cloth by Holliston, Kingsport, Tennessee.